THE TEACH YOURSELF BOOKS
EDITED BY LEONARD CUTTS

TEACH YOURSELF
CYCLING

TEACH YOURSELF

CYCLING

By
REGINALD C. SHAW

First published in Great Britain in 1953.

This edition published in Great Britain in 2017 by John Murray Learning,
an imprint of Hodder & Stoughton. An Hachette UK company.

British Library Cataloguing in Publication Data: a catalogue
record for this title is available from the British Library.

Hardback: 978 1 473 66421 0
eBook: 978 1 473 66419 7

1

Cover image © Getty Images
Printed and bound in Great Britain by CPI Group (UK) Ltd., Croydon, CR0 4YY.

John Murray Learning policy is to use papers that are natural, renewable
and recyclable products and made from wood grown in sustainable forests.
The logging and manufacturing processes are expected to conform to
the environmental regulations of the country of origin.

Carmelite House
50 Victoria Embankment
London EC4Y 0DZ
www.hodder.co.uk

Also available
in ebook

PREFACE

THERE must be something like ten million bicycles in more or less regular use in Britain at the present time. Generally speaking, they are good bicycles too, for modern machines are well designed, well made, and easy to ride.

Yet only a small proportion of the millions of people who ride cycles do so for pleasure. The others have no idea what they are missing, and it is hoped that this book will be useful as an introduction to the simplest and happiest of all outdoor recreations, by showing the casual riders of cycles the way to enjoyment and health.

At the same time it is hoped that the chapters dealing with road usage will be useful to all cyclists, whether they ride for pleasure or merely for convenience, and help them to attain the highest possible standard of roadmanship.

ACKNOWLEDGMENT

THE publishers gratefully acknowledge permission to include eight pen drawings by Frank Patterson, originally published in *The C.T.C. Gazette*.

CONTENTS

CHAPTER I

CYCLISTS AND BIKE-RIDERS

Riding a bicycle is so easy that almost everybody can do it. There is nothing to it—nothing to learn and nothing to teach—certainly not enough to fill a book like this.

That, at least, is what most people think. Having already learned to ride a bicycle—that is to say, to sit on it, balance it, steer it, and make the thing go—they are quite satisfied in their own minds that they know all there is to know about cycling. It is a cheap and easy way of getting about, so long as you do not try to do too much of it.

Most of the millions of bike-riders in this country think like that. A few hundred thousand cyclists disagree with them, but who are they among so many?

There is a tremendous difference between the point of view of the enthusiastic cyclist and that of the ordinary rider of a bicycle. The only thing they have in common is the belief that the bicycle is a cheap and easy means of transport; but the cyclist knows that that is not by any means the whole story: it is no more than the opening chapter.

The handful of enthusiastic cyclists are the only ones who really know how easy and very enjoyable cycling can be. The bike-riders do not know; they have no idea at all. In fact they haven't yet learned to ride.

Admittedly they have picked up the trick of balancing and propelling a bicycle, but that is nothing. What they have not learned is the easy, efficient, effective style of riding that makes all the difference between "shoving a bike around" and the delightful activity that really deserves to be called cycling.

Cycling is not just riding a bicycle, and the average

rider of a bicycle does not know much about it. He does not even know how useful his bicycle can be for getting about—really getting about, and not just pootling around.

No doubt the bike-rider knows how handy his bike is for running down to the shops, or to the tennis-courts, or even for going to and from work (so long as it isn't too far away and the weather isn't too bad). But, good heavens! says the cyclist, you can't call that getting about.

There are times when the bike-rider himself begins to suspect that he may be missing something, after all. When he sees cyclists riding easily up hills which he himself always has to walk it makes him think. And when he hears—as he must do now and again—of people who go off cycling for miles and miles, thoroughly enjoying it, and evidently not getting so tired after a hundred miles as he himself would be after fifteen or twenty, he cannot help feeling that he would like to know the explanation.

Perhaps he tries to stifle his suspicions that there may be something in it, after all, by saying that those other people, the keen cyclists and the riders who seem to find it so easy to climb hills, must be the athletic type, or younger than he is, or more in practice, or probably that they've got better bicycles. He cannot explain it all away like that, though.

Of course a young athlete in perfect training and riding a first-class modern light-weight bicycle can do better than a flabby, middle-aged rider on a cumbersome old roadster, but even the best of present-day cycles (and nowadays they are easier to propel than they have ever been) will not change the unskilled bike-rider into even a passable cyclist. In fact, the skilled cyclist—the one who has learned the difference between mere bike-riding and real cycling—will always be able to put up a better show on an out-of-date bike than the mere bike-rider can achieve even when he is mounted on the

The CASTLE
Castle Rising
Once a seaport fortress.

most up-to-the-minute light-weight with every modern refinement.

It is not a question of age, physique or money. It is entirely a matter of skill and knowledge—something that can be learned.

You can teach yourself cycling.

CHAPTER II

SECRETS OF EASY CYCLING

IF you are going to teach yourself cycling, obviously you ought to have a bicycle and be able to ride it. At this stage it does not matter very much what kind of bike it is, but later on, when you know more about cycling, you will no doubt want to get hold of a really good machine.

By then, however, you will have learned not only how to make good use of a good bicycle, but also how to recognise a good bicycle when you see one, and especially how to choose the best bicycle for your particular requirements. Until then, almost "any old iron" will do to learn on.

Learning to Ride

Perhaps, though, we ought not to assume that you can already ride a bicycle. You may be one of those very rare people who did not learn when they were children. In that case at least you will not have picked up the abominable habit of pedalling with your instep, so there will be one fault the fewer for you to correct.

To learn to ride, you do not need anybody's help. You will be better off on your own.

Just borrow a bicycle that is not too big. Lower the saddle so that when you are sitting on it you can put both feet fairly and squarely on the ground. Then find a nice quiet road—preferably a gentle hill. Take up a position on the left-hand side of the road, facing downhill, so that if there does happen to be any traffic about you will not be a bigger nuisance than you need be at this stage of your cycling career.

Now take hold of the handle-bar grips, after making sure that the brakes work and that you know which lever operates the back one. That is the one you are going to use, and it should be on the left-hand side; but if it is not, do not worry for the present.

All you have to do now is to push off with your feet. If you are on a hill, just let your feet scrape along the ground until you have got the feel of the bike. Then try lifting them just clear of the ground, so that you can restore your balance quickly by putting them down again. And try not to use the brake until you really do want to stop; the faster you go, the easier it is, so long as you do not let the cycle get out of control.

If you are not on a hill you will have to push off with your feet and then use them to scoot along.

In either case do not bother about the pedals until you have found out how to balance the bike. It will not be long before you can manage to travel several yards without having to put your feet down, and soon after that you will discover the trick of recovering your balance without putting your feet down at all. You do it by manipulating the handle-bar, but the knack will come naturally and more quickly if you do not try to think it out and do it deliberately.

When you have learned the trick of balancing and steering, you can put your feet on the pedals and start turning them round. Now, at any rate, you are a bike-rider.

Saddle Position

While you were learning to balance the bike, you had the saddle really low, because that gave you a good position for scooting. It is not very good for pedalling, though, and now that you have begun to master your machine you will want to fix the saddle where it will allow you to make the best use of your legs.

Making good use of the legs is one of the main factors in efficient and easy cycling, but it is not entirely a question of saddle position. For the moment, however, it is the saddle position that you are thinking about.

You have a good deal of scope, as you can raise or lower the saddle and also move it backwards and forwards.

First of all you have to make sure that the saddle is not so high that you cannot comfortably reach the pedals when they are in the bottom position. At the same time you do not want to be seated so low that your legs are always uncomfortably bent. You cannot put all your strength into your pedalling if your legs are restricted like that.

The best position will probably be found by fixing the saddle so that you can just put your heel on the pedal when it is at the bottom. Of course, you are not going to ride like that, but measuring your leg length in such a way ensures that when you are pedalling with the broad part of your shoe on the pedal your leg will never be stretched to its full extent. You will see the advantage of that later on.

When the height of the saddle has been fixed—at least approximately—you should consider whether the saddle ought to be moved a little bit farther forwards or backwards. In this case the adjustment is not so easy to make by any rule of thumb, and quite possibly, as you learn more about cycling, you will continue to make small variations until you are finally satisfied that you have found your ideal position.

Probably, as you are not yet accustomed to long-distance riding, you will at first feel inclined to have the saddle rather near to the handle-bar grips, so that you can sit comfortably over the pedals, with your back almost vertical and your arms just resting loosely on the handle-bar.

That is the position traditionally adopted by policemen. It resembles fairly closely the cavalry position, but what may be good when riding a horse is not necessarily good for riding a bicycle. There is, in fact, an important difference between riding a horse and riding a bicycle. The rider of a bicycle has to work with his legs. His sitting position must be carefully chosen to help him to make good use of his legs—an important factor in easy cycling.

If the rider of a cycle is not going far, and if he does not mind pedalling inefficiently so long as he is comfortably seated, the policeman's posture is good enough. The bobby sits solidly over his pedals, almost all his weight being supported by the saddle, and he pedals by straightening first one leg and then the other, letting them be carried upwards again by the rising pedals. When he comes to a hill he takes a firmer grip on the handle-bar and begins to pull on it, so that he can put more force into his pedalling, which is nothing more than a downward thrust from his thighs.

Soon after that the policeman dismounts and walks up the remainder of the hill, wheeling his bicycle nonchalantly under the gaze of the cyclists who glide past him without apparent effort. In similar circumstances anybody less afraid of losing a little dignity would probably not dismount quite so soon. Instead he would start using his weight, by transferring it from the saddle to the pedals. Standing on the pedals and going through the motions of climbing deep and steep stairs or working a treadmill, he would force the pedals down by putting all his weight first on one and then on the other.

That may not be a pretty sight, especially if the rider cannot keep his bicycle straight, and so wobbles and sways from side to side, but it does the trick—for a time. The use of brute force like that is a waste of energy, and very soon becomes tiring.

Efficient Pedalling

A far better method of pedalling is to make full use of all the available muscular energy without wasting any. That means using not only the muscles of the thighs, but also others in the lower legs and the feet themselves.

The more muscles are used, the less work each one of them has to do, and so the longer it can keep on working without getting tired. That is the fundamental prin-

ciple of good pedalling. And now you must find a
position of the saddle and handle-bar that will enable
you to put the principle into practice.

By making use of your foot- and leg-muscles as well as
those in your thighs, you will be able, when you have had
a bit of practice, to turn your pedals round and round
with your feet just as you would turn a rotary handle with
your hands.

It is worth while studying the action of a girl or woman
who is turning the handle of a sewing-machine. She
does not just grasp the handle and push it backwards

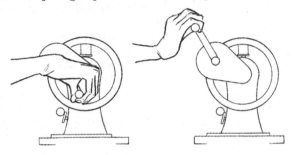

and forwards by using her arm as a kind of piston.
Instead, she makes good use of her wrist, moving her
clenched fist up and down at the joint, as the hand goes
round and round. The result is a smooth, circular
movement, whereas if she kept her wrist rigid, and only
allowed her arm to bend at the elbow- and shoulder-
joints, she would produce a series of forceful thrusts
with a pronounced rhythm.

Most people pedal like that. Moving their legs only
at the thigh- and knee-joints, and using only the thigh-
muscles, they just push the pedals down, instead of
turning them round.

To achieve the rotary movement in pedalling it is
necessary to learn to use the ankle-joint as much as
possible—quite a tiring job at first, because most of us
have let our ankles lose a good deal of their original

flexibility—and to adopt a saddle position that will enable the foot to get behind the pedal and push forwards as well as downwards.

The drawings on this page show the style of pedalling that is most efficient. It is efficient not only because it brings into use the maximum number of muscles, and so shares the effort and enables the rider to keep it up for a longer time, but also because it permits the pedaller to exert rotary pressure on the pedals over a greater part of their travel.

The actual pressure on the pedal begins just before

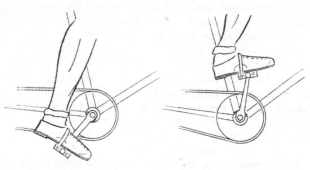

it reaches the top of its travel. At that point the foot—like the seamstress's hand—should be pointed upwards. Then, not only does the rider's leg begin to straighten, thus exerting a downwards pressure on the pedal, but at the same time the foot is pressed forwards and downwards, increasing the angle that it makes with the lower leg.

When the descending foot is somewhere about the half-way point it is in a horizontal position—the position that most riders maintain all the time—and there it begins to press backwards with the toes, while the leg itself continues to push downwards. In that way the foot keeps up the rotary movement beyond the lowest position of the pedal.

The bigger the angle through which the foot moves, in

relation to the lower leg, the more successful will be this style of pedalling, which is generally known as " ankling ". At first it will cause aches in muscles above the instep, behind the ankle, and in the calves; but eventually the aches will disappear, the ankle-joints will become more flexible than before, and the effort required to pedal will become noticeably less than it used to be in the same circumstances.

This, the most efficient style of pedalling, is possible only if the saddle is in the appropriate position behind the bottom bracket. The exact situation depends on the rider's physique, and will probably not be found immediately, as even small variations may have unexpectedly great influences on pedalling proficiency.

If the saddle is too far behind the pedals, the rider will find it easy to press forward at the top of the pedalling stroke, but difficult to keep up the foot-pressure towards the bottom. If he is seated too far forwards, he will feel hampered at the top of the stroke, not being able, apparently, to point his feet upwards as much as he should, but at the bottom of the stroke he will find it easy to " paw " the pedal round.

When practising this style of pedalling for the first time, it is advisable to do it on an uphill gradient, so that there will be enough resistance in the pedals to make the rider have to press really hard. Hard, slow pedalling in circumstances like that is the best kind of training for the development of ankling technique, which, when it has been acquired, will be of tremendous benefit in hill-climbing and in battles against strong head-winds.

Handle-bar Position

If the rider who is practising ankling for the first time is mounted on a machine with one of the old-fashioned upturned handle-bars, he will almost certainly find that his hands are too near the saddle. He will have a natural tendency to take hold of the bar at its most forward point—the centre—and pull against it so that he can make the best use of his legs.   He will, in fact, become very conscious of the disadvantage of that type of handle-bar, which sweeps backwards too much.

UPTURNED BAR   DROPPED BAR   FLAT BAR

The important feature of any handle-bar is the position it provides for the rider's hands, and it does not really matter whether the bar itself is curved upwards or down-

Comfortable and Efficient

wards, so long as the grips are suitably placed. As will be seen from the diagram on the left, it is possible for the rider of a bicycle with a raised, a flat, or a slightly dropped handle-bar to obtain exactly the same riding position— that is to say, the same relationship between the positions

STEERING IS HAMPERED BY ELBOWS

Ungainly and Inefficient

of handle-bar, saddle and bottom bracket (where the pedal-cranks are attached to the chainwheel spindle).

It is, in fact, the riding position that matters, and if the rider prefers a machine with a slightly raised bar, such as the North Road upturned, or a dropped one like the same bar reversed, or even a flat, that is entirely a personal matter for him to decide as he wishes. What is far more important is that the handle-bar should enable him to lean comfortably on it when cruising along, thus taking part of the weight of his body on his wrists, and to pull on it when he wants to put the maximum effort into his pedalling. The old type of upturned handle-bar is no good for that, and it encourages the rider to let his arms rest loosely on the grips when he is not actually pulling on them, and induces him to sit bolt upright on his saddle in the policeman's posture, which, as we have seen, is not suitable for anything but quite short rides.

The three types of handle-bar so far illustrated are probably the most generally useful of all, and there is no important difference between them, as the hand position

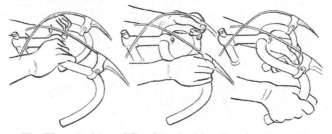

The Three Positions Offered by the Most Popular Type of Dropped Handle-bar

is identical in every case. Handle-bars of that kind make it possible for the rider to select a really good position for the hands. Some riders like, however, to have more than one position available. Many tourists, for instance, insist on having bars of the conventional dropped pattern because they provide three alternative positions for the hands—on the grips for times when it is desired to exert the maximum effort, as in hill-climbing or facing a headwind; on the part of the bar immediately above the grips, for easier conditions; and on the transverse part of the bar when the rider is temporarily adopting something like the policeman's posture for a change.

For racing, of course, a dropped bar is essential, in order to give the rider as streamlined a position as possible, and so cut down wind resistance, but it is regrettable that so many young riders nowadays adopt an absurdly exaggerated racing position for normal riding. They do harm to themselves and to the good name of cycling.

Whatever kind of handle-bar is adopted, the rider should remember that the position of his hands and the inclination of the upper part of his body when riding also

Racing Position

have an influence on the choice of a suitable saddle. Anyone sitting on a saddle in the policeman's posture is supporting his weight on a part of the pelvis that is fairly wide in comparison with the part that takes the weight when he leans forward in something like a racing position. In the " sit-up " attitude he needs a fairly wide saddle, but the same saddle will not do for the racing position, because it will interfere with the free movement of the thighs and probably cause chafing against the saddle-flaps.

CHAPTER III

THE PURPOSE OF GEARING

IT is surprising how many people who quite frequently ride bicycles have no idea what gearing means and how it affects them. It is also surprising how many cycle manufacturers are still marketing bicycles that are too highly geared.

In this country the gearing of a bicycle is indicated in an unusual and rather interesting way. Another system is used on the continent of Europe, but neither is the normal mechanical method.

It is easy to show that a bicycle is geared up. When the pedal-cranks are revolved the back wheel turns more quickly than the chainwheel, according to the relative sizes of the chainwheel (to which the pedal-cranks are attached) and the rear sprocket (which is attached to the back wheel). Chainwheel and rear sprocket are connected by means of the cycle chain, and because the rear sprocket is smaller than the chainwheel it revolves more than once every time the chainwheel makes one complete revolution.

If the chainwheel is three times as big as the rear sprocket, the sprocket will do three turns for every one made by the chainwheel. In that case the gearing would normally be expressed as a ratio of one-to-three ($1:3$), and to indicate the gear of any bicycle it would only be necessary to quote the relative sizes of chainwheel and sprocket, which may be conveniently expressed by the number of teeth on them.

A 48-tooth chainwheel and a 16-tooth sprocket would thus give a gear of $16:48$ or $1:3$. Suppose, however, that the gear were $18:42$. It would then be less easy to comprehend and compare with, say, $21:48$ or $19:44$, though in practice there is little difference between them.

And who could say without calculation whether 16 : 40 was higher or lower than 20 : 50? They are in fact identical, and might be expressed as 1 : 2.5.

From the cyclist's point of view the normal method of indicating gearing is not very convenient. The cyclist is not so much interested in knowing how many times his back wheel revolves every time he turns the pedals round. What he wants to know is how hard (or easy) a particular bicycle will be to push, as compared with another, in given circumstances, and that depends on the distance a bicycle will travel every time the pedals make one complete revolution.

On the Continent gearing is, in fact, expressed in terms of distance travelled for every revolution of the chainwheel and that means, of course, that the size of the back wheel has to be taken into account. The bigger the back wheel, the greater the distance it will travel for every revolution. If, for instance, the 48-tooth chainwheel and 16-tooth sprocket (giving the 1 : 3 ratio) were fitted to a bicycle with 26-inch wheels, the gear would be said to be three times the circumference of the wheel (that is to say, the circumference multiplied by the gearing expressed in the ordinary way) or 6 yards 2 feet 5 inches. In the metric system that result is somewhat less formidable (6·14 metres), but even so the need to convert the diameter of the wheel into its circumference makes the calculation unnecessarily complicated.

A simpler system is used in this country, where the gearing is not expressed as the effective circumference of the rear wheel but as its diameter. It is, in fact, a relic of the days of the old penny farthing, when the pedals were directly connected to the driving-wheel and the significant measurement of a bicycle was the diameter of that wheel. It indicated not only the gearing, as we now use the term, but also the size of the bicycle itself. Only a big rider could bestride a bicycle with a big driving-wheel, but nowadays there is no relationship between bicycle size and gearing; a big rider may have a big machine with a little gear.

GEAR TABLE FOR 26-INCH WHEELS

Gears are expressed in the British (roman type) and Continental (italic) systems

No. of teeth on rear sprocket	No. of teeth on chainwheel					
	36	38	40	42	44	46
14	66·8 *5·25*	70·5 *5·54*	74·2 *5·84*	78 *6·12*	81·7 *6·42*	85·4 *6·71*
15	62·4 *4·90*	65·9 *5·17*	69·3 *5·45*	72·8 *5·72*	76·3 *5·99*	79·7 *6·26*
16	58·5 *4·59*	61·7 *4·85*	65 *5·11*	68·2 *5·36*	71·5 *5·62*	74·7 *5·87*
17	55 *4·32*	58·1 *4·56*	61·2 *4·8*	64·2 *5·04*	67·3 *5·29*	70·2 *5·53*
18	52 *4·08*	54·9 *4·31*	57·8 *4·54*	60·6 *4·76*	63·5 *4·99*	66·4 *5·22*
19	49·2 *3·87*	52 *4·08*	54·7 *4·29*	57·5 *4·51*	60·2 *4·73*	62·9 *4·94*
20	46·8 *3·68*	49·4 *3·88*	52 *4·08*	54·6 *4·29*	57·2 *4·49*	59·8 *4·69*
21	44·5 *3·50*	47 *3·69*	49·5 *3·89*	52 *4·08*	54·5 *4·28*	56·9 *4·47*
22	42·5 *3·34*	44·9 *3·53*	47·2 *3·71*	49·6 *3·89*	52 *4·08*	54·3 *4·27*
23	40·6 *3·19*	42·9 *3·37*	45·2 *3·55*	47·5 *3·73*	49·7 *3·91*	52 *4·08*
24	39 *3·06*	41·2 *3·23*	43·3 *3·40*	45·5 *3·57*	47·7 *3·74*	49·8 *3·91*
26	36 *2·83*	38 *2·98*	40 *3·14*	42 *3·29*	44 *3·46*	46 *3·61*
28	33·4 *2·63*	35·3 *2·77*	37·1 *2·92*	39 *3·06*	40·8 *3·21*	42·7 *3·35*

In the modern English system of expressing gears, if the 48-tooth chainwheel and the 16-tooth sprocket are connected to a 26-inch cycle wheel they are said to give

The historic Court House
Long Crendon

a gear of 78 inches, or a theoretical diameter three times the actual diameter $\left(\frac{48}{16} \times 26\right)$. Similarly the 18 : 42, the 21 : 48 and the 19 : 44 combinations give gears of 60·6, 59·4 and 60·2.

That method of expression makes it easy to compare one gear with another, even when they are obtained by different combinations of chainwheel, sprocket and rear wheel. A table of gears expressed in the British and the Continental ways is given on page 26.

Why should cyclists want to take such a profound interest in the gearing of their mounts? What effect has gearing on their riding and on the amount of work they must put into their pedalling?

Gearing cannot reduce the amount of work to be done. The cyclist who rides up a hill on his bicycle will have to transport the weight of himself and his bicycle from the bottom of the hill to the top, no matter how his machine is geared. The work to be done cannot be changed, but it can be made easier or harder by the way in which it is done.

Everybody knows that a hundredweight of sand can be lifted three feet by a small child if the child is given a shovel of suitable size and allowed to take his own time over the job. The same child could not lift the sand in one heave, though a stronger adult might. And an older child would be able to lift the sand in a smaller number of shovelfuls if he used a bigger shovel. But they would all—children and adults alike—have done the same amount of work in the end, having lifted one hundredweight three feet, though they had taken very different lengths of time to do it.

The principle is the same when the job to be done is the lifting of a bicycle and its rider to the top of a hill. If the rider is hefty, and the bicycle is geared fairly high, he will be able to take himself and the bike to the top of the hill in a comparatively small number of revolutions of the chainwheel. If, however, he is feeble in physique, he will still be able to get to the top of the hill, provided his cycle has a low enough gear, so that he can increase the number of chainwheel revolutions. The actual cycle wheels will, of course, revolve the same number of times between the bottom of the hill and the top whatever the gear, but with the lower gear a single revolution of the chainwheel will push the bike a shorter distance, and so do a smaller part of the work of getting machine and rider to the top.

In such circumstances the feeble rider will take longer to make the climb (unless, of course, he is foolish enough to tire himself out by pedalling at a faster rate than the hefty fellow). He will, in fact, have done the job in a greater number of " shovelfuls ", each being smaller than the hefty fellow is capable of lifting.

The whole purpose of cycle gearing is to enable the rider to do the work that has to be done at a rate which suits him in the existing circumstances. Intelligently used, it is a great help, enabling comparatively weak riders to do long rides, but wrongly used it can make cycling hard work. Unfortunately, quite a number of riders are nowadays pushing around bikes that are geared too high. Those are the real push-bikes.

Sooner or later, therefore, in the pleasant task of teaching yourself cycling, you will have to decide what gear will suit you best for normal riding, and then settle to your own satisfaction the question of what other gears you ought to have in reserve to meet the conditions you are likely to encounter during your riding.

If, for instance, you live in flattish country and have no wish to go adventuring where there are mountains (but you will, you know, when you have really taught yourself something about cycling), then a bike with a single gear of between 65 and 70 will probably suit you very well. Older people may find it advisable to go below 65, and some energetic youths may reasonably adopt a 73 or 75, but for most people in the circumstances mentioned the 65–70 range will be adequate.

If, on the other hand, your cycling is going to include some of the famous mountain passes on the Continent, you will probably decide, when you are experienced enough to make such a decision, that you ought to have a bottom gear of 35, or even lower. Even if you never go into hilly districts, if you add a sidecar to your bicycle, thus increasing the amount of work to be done, you may find it worth while lowering the gear.

The ideal would be an infinitely variable gear, to meet infinitely varying conditions; but that is not yet attainable. We can, however, get very near it in practice, as you will see later.

In the meantime work out the gear of the machine you are using by the following formula:

$$\text{Gear} = \frac{\text{Number of teeth on chainwheel}}{\text{Number of teeth on sprocket}} \times \frac{\text{Diameter of}}{\text{rear wheel}} \text{ in inches}$$

Your experience in using that gear will help you later on to decide what gear you should specify for the ideal bicycle you will eventually want to buy.

CHAPTER IV

ROAD RULES AND REGULATIONS

Now that you have taught yourself to ride a bicycle and you understand the theories of efficient pedalling, you will naturally want to get as much cycling practice as possible.

The place for that is out on the open road, but before you set off to mingle with the millions of other people with whom you have to share the British roads, there is just one more item in your cycling education that you ought to tackle. You must learn the rules of road-usage and how to apply them.

There is one important difference between the basic principles of good road-usage and the fundamental theories of efficient cycling. If you are negligent in applying the principles of pedalling, you will be the only one to suffer, and in any case it is entirely open to you to decide for yourself whether you think it worth while making the effort to become a good pedaller or not. But you cannot look at the rules of good road-usage in that way; they do not merely concern you, but affect everybody else on the roads as well, and they cannot be considered on a " take-it-or-leave-it " basis.

You are going to share the roads with other people, many of whom will be travelling much faster than you. Only if you, and they, agree to keep to the rules in all circumstances can you, and they, use the roads with the greatest possible convenience all round.

The rules of the road are not merely the laws and regulations that govern the use of the roads, but they also include all the principles of safe and courteous road-usage on which the Highway Code is based. Though some of the rules are laws and can be enforced, whereas others have only semi-legal force, they should all be accepted and adopted by everybody to whom they apply.

Let us take the laws and regulations first, starting with the age-old common-law rule of " keep to the left ".

There was a time, in the early days of cycling, when the keep-left rule was practically the only one that mattered. Overtaking and passing were the only circumstances calling for any form of control, and all that was necessary was to make sure that on those occasions the drivers concerned knew which side of the road to take.

Traffic was so sparse and travelled so slowly that most of today's difficulties never arose. The cyclist wanting to turn from one road to another on the right, for instance, did not have first of all to cross a stream of faster-moving vehicles going in the same direction as himself and then another one coming the opposite way. That, however, is a common situation nowadays, and rules have had to be devised to meet it, so that everybody involved can go about his business with the least delay and danger.

The old-time cyclist used to turn to the right as he thought fit, guided only by his common sense, but the cyclist of today often has to do it in circumstances where there are strictly enforceable rules of priority.

Priority Principle

Priority is, in fact, the first principle of modern traffic control. Where the old-fashioned " free enter-prise " would be dangerous, and where drivers and cyclists cannot reasonably be left to sort themselves out on the old keep-left principle, it is usual nowadays for a system of definite priorities to be adopted.

It may be established permanently by giving all the traffic on one road definite precedence over that on another. In such cases one road is designated a major road, and traffic entering it has to do so without impeding or endangering the traffic already on it. If the entrance to the major road is controlled by a " halt " sign the traffic coming from the minor road must actually stop and wait until it is safe to cross the line that marks the entry to the major road.

In many cases, however, the traffic on the minor road entering a major road is not compelled to come to an absolute stop, although it is still bound to concede priority to the traffic on the major road. In such instances, instead of a " halt " sign, a " slow " sign is set up to control the entrance to the major road.

A permanent priority system of that kind can only be adopted if the traffic on one road is obviously and always more important than that on the other road, which can therefore reasonably be described as a minor road. Where roads of roughly equal importance join or cross one another, and the traffic on them is heavy enough to call for control, a system of alternating priorities is usually set up. The traffic is given priority first on one road and then on the other.

This system of control may be applied either by installations of traffic lights or by the use of traffic-control policemen. In either case cyclists and other drivers of vehicles must obey the light-signals or the signals given by the policemen. If they do not they can be prosecuted, and a cyclist should remember that he must obey signals whether he is riding his bicycle or merely wheeling it. In either case he is, in the eyes of the law, the driver of a carriage.

Where roads of roughly equal importance cross one another, but where the traffic on them is not heavy enough to justify holding it up on one road to let that on the other go forward without hindrance, a third system of control is frequently applied. In this case the intention is not to stop the traffic and make it give way to that coming from another direction, but to bring all traffic down to a speed at which the individual drivers can sort themselves out. This is done by the construc-

B

tion of roundabouts, obstacles which drivers cannot negotiate without reducing speed.

At roundabouts in Britain none of the converging streams of traffic has priority over the others, but in some countries there is a general rule that traffic coming from one side or the other must be given the right of way. In France and Switzerland at the present time it is traffic coming from the right (that is to say, the near side) which has priority, but there are many advocates of a change to an " off-side rule ". The " off-side rule " has frequently been advocated for adoption in this country, but up to the present it has not found favour. For us, of course, the off side is the right, and if such a rule were adopted in this country, it would mean that traffic entering a roundabout would always have to give priority to the traffic already circulating in it.

Generally speaking, no class of road-user has priority over another in this country, but an important exception to that generalisation is the privileged position of pedestrians in certain circumstances. They have priority over all forms of vehicular traffic (which includes cycles, of course) on pedestrian crossings that are not controlled by traffic lights or police. At controlled crossings pedestrians should cross only when vehicular traffic is held up, and should look out for vehicles turning corners. The drivers and cyclists must similarly watch for pedestrians who may be crossing when the traffic lights or policeman give the release signal, and they should give way to pedestrians crossing the road into which they are turning.

Cycling Laws

Quite apart from the enforceable rules so far mentioned, which all intelligent people accept as a necessary and valuable aid to free movement on the roads, there are several others, equally enforceable, which apply specifically to cyclists.

It is an offence against the law (the Road Traffic Act

of 1934) for a cyclist to carry passengers on his cycle unless it is " constructed or adapted for the carriage of more than one person ". The law does not say what "constructed or adapted " means, but obviously a tandem bicycle is constructed for the carriage of more than one person. It is also generally accepted that the special seats sold for attachment to bicycles so that children can then be carried on them are also legal adaptations. In other cases whether a machine has been " constructed or adapted " will depend on the view taken by the magistrates.

It is illegal under another of the Road Traffic Acts (that of 1930) for a cyclist to hang on to motor vehicles or trailers for the purpose of being drawn along, unless he has lawful authority or reasonable cause to do so. If therefore a cyclist hangs on to a stationary vehicle in a traffic block he is not breaking the law, but if he still hangs on when the vehicle begins to move he is committing an offence, unless he can show that he has lawful authority to hang on or can prove that he had reasonable cause for doing so.

Because it is legally established that a cyclist is the driver of a carriage, it is illegal for him to take his cycle on to a footway or a footpath by the side of a road. That is to say, he must not leave the carriage-way and use the footway. Under the same Act of Parliament (the Highways Act of 1835) a cyclist, as the driver of a carriage, may be prosecuted if he drives furiously so as to endanger the life or limb of anyone, including himself.

At the moment there are no laws compelling bells or brakes to be fitted to cycles. The Minister of Transport has power, however, under the Road Traffic Act of 1934 to make regulations prescribing the number, nature and use of brakes on cycles, and under the 1930 Road Traffic Act he has power to make regulations prescribing the manner in which cyclists shall give warning of their approach. No Minister of Transport has yet made use of those powers.

Lighting Regulations

The position is somewhat similar with regard to the
warnings that have to be fitted to cycles when they are
used on the roads during the hours of darkness. The
Road Transport Lighting (Cycles) Act of 1945 laid it
down that every cycle on the roads after dark should be
fitted with a red rear light, a red reflector and a " white
surface ".   It was left to the Minister of Transport to say
when the need to carry reflectors and white surfaces
should come into force and also to prescribe regulations
governing the carrying of the white surfaces.   Up to the
present he has not fixed a day for making reflectors and
white surfaces compulsory.   Until he does so a cycle that
is used on the roads in the dark is complying with the
law so long as it is fitted with a red rear light and a
white front light.

The white front light is necessary under the Road
Transport Lighting Act of 1927, which relates not only
to cycles but to other vehicles as well.   The other
vehicles have to carry two white front lights, but bicycles
are specifically " let off " with one, unless they have a
sidecar attached.   In that case a white front light must
be carried on the sidecar as well, but there is no need to
fit an extra rear light.

If a cyclist has trouble with his lights when he is out
riding after dark, he is allowed to go on his way without
lights so long as he walks and wheels his bicycle as near
as possible to the left-hand edge of the carriage-way.
The only circumstance in which an unlighted cycle can
be allowed to be motionless on the road after dark is when
it has been stopped in order to comply with any traffic
signal or direction or owing to the exigencies of the
traffic.   Even then it must be as near as possible to the
left-hand edge of the carriage-way.

A cycle must not be left on the road in the dark if it is
not carrying lights.   Similarly if a cycle is fitted with a
dynamo lighting-set, which gives a light only when the

cycle is moving, the rider must take up a position on the left-hand side of the road when he stops. He cannot therefore do what he would normally do when about to turn to the right at traffic lights. In ordinary circumstances he would come to a halt near the middle of the road and then move off as soon as he got the signal to do so. If he did that with an unlighted bicycle he would be breaking the law. So the user of a dynamo lighting-set must always keep to the left of the road unless he has a standby battery which he can bring into use when he stops.

The lighting laws relate to vehicles that are used on the road " during the hours of darkness ", which begin at what is commonly called lighting-up time. Lighting-up time is based on the time of sunset, but the relationship between lighting-up time and sunset time is not constant throughout the year. In winter—that is to say, between the first Sunday in October and the third Sunday in April—lighting-up time is half an hour after sunset time and " lights-off time " is half an hour before sunrise. Throughout the rest of the year lighting-up time is an hour after sunset and lights-off time an hour before sunrise.

CHAPTER V

ROADMANSHIP

No one can consider himself a good cyclist unless he is also a good road-user. Roadmanship is, in fact, an essential part of cycling, and in teaching yourself cycling you must aim at acquiring a high degree of roadmanship.

The essence of roadmanship is (1) knowing what to do in all circumstances, (2) being able always to do what is required, and (3) doing it. The enforceable road rules discussed in the preceding chapter are the foundation of good road-usage, but they are not by any means the whole of it. No less important are the rules set out in the Highway Code, which, though only a very small number of the rules have full legal force, is accepted and adopted by all people who wish to use the roads in a safe and courteous manner. The Highway Code precepts are, in fact, the good manners of the road.

There are two main principles underlying the rules in the Highway Code. The first is that each road-user should recognise that all others have as much right to use the roads as he has. The second is that no road-user should do any unexpected action.

It seems obvious when put into words that a cyclist should never suddenly shoot off to the right without thinking of the traffic behind him and any that may be coming towards him. Yet that is the commonest fault of those who have not acquired the necessary degree of roadmanship.

What should a cyclist do if, when riding along a busy road, he wishes to turn to the right? Let us go through the whole manœuvre in detail, because it is not only important in itself, but it also exemplifies very well the spirit of the Highway Code.

Suppose, therefore, a cyclist is riding along a busy road, keeping quite near to the left-hand edge of the carriage-way, so that the faster traffic going in his direction can pass him without interference. At the other side of the road a stream of traffic is going in the opposite direction. Ahead of the cyclist, but on the other side of the road, is a side turning into which he intends to ride.

If the cyclist is not yet completely master of his machine, and cannot turn round in the saddle so as to look behind him without causing his bicycle to swerve

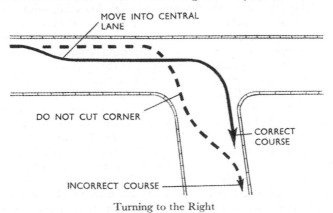

Turning to the Right

towards the middle of the road, he will continue until he comes to the part of the road on which he is riding that is opposite to the side turning. There he will pull up and wait for a break in the stream of traffic that is overtaking him. Then he can walk or ride to the middle of the road and wait there for an opportunity to cross the stream of traffic coming in the other direction.

If, however, the cyclist is more experienced and more skilful, he will begin the manœuvre of turning to the right long before he reaches the actual junction. First of all, when he is still some fifty or sixty yards away (the exact distance will depend on his speed at the time) he will look behind him to find a suitable opening in the stream of vehicles passing him. As the opening approaches he will signal his intention to turn by putting out his right arm. The signal will probably have been expected by the drivers of the other vehicles who have seen him looking behind, but in any case the cyclist will make the signal as clear and unmistakable as possible. A casual flipping of the right wrist at about hip level is not good enough.

A clear signal having been given, the cyclist now moves through the break in the stream of overtaking traffic and continues to ride down the middle of the road towards the point where the side turning comes in. All the time he is holding out his right arm, and the drivers of overtaking traffic know that they can safely pass him on the inside.

At the junction, if there is a suitable break in the stream of approaching traffic, the cyclist can turn into the side street, going over to the left-hand side of it, and not cutting the corner. If, however, the approaching stream of traffic is unbroken, the cyclist must come to a halt in the middle of the road. He can do so without danger and without interfering with other traffic because he has made clear his intention and given adequate warning in good time to other road-users. Moreover, he will not try to force a way through the stream of approaching traffic until it is safe for him to do so. The approaching traffic has, in fact, the right of way, but in any case no capable cyclist will object to waiting his turn in such circumstances.

Throughout the manœuvre we have just been discussing the cyclist made his intentions perfectly clear to the other road-users, and did nothing that would cause them to swerve or brake suddenly. Unfortunately, not all cycle-riders are so punctilious in their conduct on the roads, and a considerable proportion of the accidents in which cyclists are involved must be attributed to their own failure to attain the necessary degree of road-

CHILDS WICKHAM CROSS
Gloucestershire.

manship.   Admittedly the consequences of the accidents
are generally made more serious because a motor vehicle
is also involved, but the presence of motor vehicles is a
factor which every intelligent cyclist will count upon in
modern circumstances.   It is quite possible for all types
of road-user to travel in perfect safety if they will
practise the rules applicable to themselves.

When making a left-hand turn, the cyclist's chief
concern is not so much to make his intention obvious

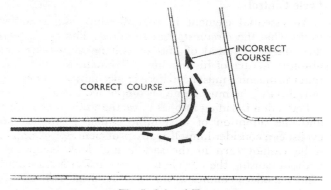

The Left-hand Turn

to other road-users as to avoid swinging out towards
the centre line of the road.   If, as he approaches the
side turning on the left, he keeps a reasonable distance
from the left-hand edge of the carriage-way of the road
in which he is riding, overtaking traffic will not be
inconvenienced whether he continues to go straight
ahead or takes the left-hand turn.   There is not, therefore, the same need to give a signal before turning to the
left as there is before making a turn to the right.   The
intelligent cyclist will, however, give a signal if he thinks
that it will help some other road-user.   It may be, for
example, that the driver of a motor vehicle coming
in the opposite direction also intends to turn into the
same side road.   In that case the driver, assuming that

the cyclist intends to continue in a straight line, will wait for him to pass before beginning to make his right-hand turn. If, however, the cyclist, seeing the intention of the motor driver, lets him know that he, too, is turning into the side road, it may be that the driver will be able, in perfect safety, to enter the side road without waiting. Similarly, a signal given by the cyclist may be helpful to the driver of a car waiting to come out of the side road.

Cycle Control

An essential element in roadmanship is the ability to do what the circumstances require. The cyclist can do what is required of him only if he is at all times absolute master of his machine. That means not only that the machine must be in perfect mechanical condition, but also that he must be an accomplished rider.

Perfection in riding implies more than skilful pedalling and the adoption of a suitable riding position. No cyclist can consider himself really proficient, for example, if he cannot turn in the saddle and look backwards without causing the bicycle to swerve towards the right. Under modern conditions this is an essential skill, and is easily acquired after a little practice. It is quite a simple balancing feat in which the cyclist has to adjust his weight towards the left as he turns towards the right. Before he turns his shoulders to the right he should ease his grasp on the right handle-bar grip and at the same time take a slightly firmer hold with his left hand. It may, in fact, be even better for him to remove the right hand altogether, especially as he will probably wish to make a signal with it. If, while this is being done, the rider resists the natural tendency to lean the upper part of his body slightly towards the right, he should be able to maintain a perfectly straight course in the forward direction while he is looking behind.

Skilful control of the cycle also helps very much when the rider is turning to the left. In that case he will find it an advantage to exaggerate the inward inclination

of the bicycle itself and counter it to some extent by
slightly inclining his body to the right. The result will
be a close turn made with greater safety than if both
machine and rider were inclining in the same direction
at the same angle, especially on a wet road.

A proficient cyclist always shows skill and intelligence
in the use of his brakes. He never applies them violently
and skids his machine to a standstill. On wet days, if
his bicycle is fitted with rim-brakes, he makes allowance
for the time that will be lost when he applies his brakes
because they will not act until the film of moisture
between the rim and brake-blocks has been removed by
friction. Similarly, the intelligent rider does not apply
his brakes when going round a corner on a wet surface if
he can possibly avoid doing so. And he never uses the
front brake alone before applying the other one.

Detective Sense

There is one element in the cultivation of roadmanship which only intelligent imagination combined with
experience can produce. It may be described as the
acquisition of a detective sense, which gives the rider
advance warning of things that are going to happen and
prevents him from being taken by surprise.

This detective sense is best explained by example.
Suppose, for instance, a cyclist is riding along a street in
a busy city. A bus passes him and pulls up a little
distance ahead. The cyclist then moves out to pass the
bus, but when he is just about amidships the bus sets off
again, and because a car has come up behind the bus,
the cyclist finds himself uncomfortably isolated in the
middle of the traffic.

If the bus had not set off until he had passed it and
pulled in again to the left-hand side of the carriage-way,
the cyclist would, of course, have been quite safe and
happy. He did not expect the bus to set off so soon. A
more observant rider, however, might have noticed that
there was only one passenger waiting to get on the bus

when it stopped and that the conductor was about to give the starting signal just as the cyclist moved out to pass the stationary bus. In that case he would have decided that his best course was to wait for a moment behind the stationary bus.

There are countless ways in which the cultivation of this power of observation and deduction, this detective sense, helps the cyclist to realise in advance what other people are going to do. It may warn him that a car door is likely to open as he passes it. It may warn him that children are going to run in front of a stationary car because he saw their legs underneath the car as he approached it.

CHAPTER VI

DIFFERENT KINDS OF BICYCLE

THE more you learn about cycling the more you appreciate what a great difference there is between a good bicycle and " any old iron ", and though, while teaching yourself cycling, it is wise to make the best use you can of whatever machine you already possess, the time will come when you will want to buy just the bike to suit you perfectly.

Too many people buy cycles that are not really suitable for them. They do not realise, in fact, what a difference there is between one type of machine and another, because superficially there is a family likeness that is quite deceptive.

Before anybody buys a cycle he should be sure in his own mind how he is going to use it. It may be that his cycling will be limited to one particular kind of activity, but, on the other hand, the machine he is going to buy may have to fulfil quite a number of different purposes.

Most people will readily understand that there must be a considerable difference between a bicycle designed to be used for racing only and one that is intended to be as generally useful as possible. They may not realise, however, what a difference there is between a machine that is ideal for riding to and from work and another that is just the thing for week-end excursions with a cycling club.

There are, in fact, three distinctly different " ordinary " uses of a bicycle, and ideally the enthusiastic cyclist needs at least three different machines. In practice, however, he usually compromises with one that can be adapted as required.

It will be useful to examine in some detail the differences between the three " ordinary " uses of a bicycle.

The most common use of a bicycle is as a means of transport to and from work.   If a machine is to suit that purpose exactly it must be one that can be used in winter and summer alike, and obviously it will need to be as

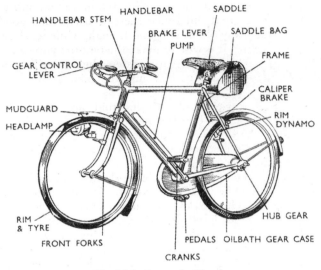

The Main Parts of a Bicycle

weatherproof and rustproof as possible.   That means not only that the " innards " must be protected as much as possible against water, mud and dust, but also that the machine should not be fitted with components or accessories that are likely to rust.

The daily distances to be ridden on the machine will be comparatively small, and the rider will be more interested in comfort, safety and reliability than in speed.   Quite probably, too, he will ride the machine when he is wearing ordinary clothes, perhaps including an overcoat or raincoat.   And if, as is quite likely, the daily journeys involve riding along busy city streets, the machine must be one that can be stopped and re-started without difficulty or acrobatics.

An experienced cyclist choosing a machine for use in such circumstances only would probably specify the following features.

1. A comparatively low frame, so that the rider can put his feet to the ground without discomfort and without dismounting whenever he has to come to a halt.

2. A flat handle-bar and a comparatively wide saddle that will give him a riding position in which, although part of his weight is carried by the handle-bar, the upper part of his body is not inclined so far forward as to be uncomfortable when wearing an overcoat or raincoat.

3. An oil-bath gear-case, to protect the chain and transmission from rain and mud.

4. Stainless-steel spokes, and as few plated parts as possible.

5. Wide enamelled mudguards that will give the maximum protection to the rider.

6. Wheels of wide section ($1\frac{3}{8}$ or $1\frac{1}{2}$ inch), fitted with tyres having a good solid tread, to reduce the risk of skidding in wet and frosty weathers.

7. Hub brakes, which are more reliable than rim brakes in wet weather, because when the rims are wet the brake blocks of rim brakes do not grip until the moisture has been removed by friction.

8. A lighting system that is as reliable as possible and needs the minimum of attention, i.e., a dynamo set.

9. A luggage carrier.

10. A variable hub gear with handle-bar control.

A machine like that would be very good indeed for riding to and from work, but it would not be the kind of mount the same cyclist would choose for long day rides either alone or with a club. For that purpose he would want something lighter and faster. In that case the main lines of the specification might be something like this.

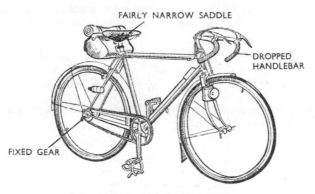

A Typical Machine for Club Riding

1. A good-quality light-weight frame.

2. A dropped handle-bar, giving a fairly forward position, and a fairly narrow saddle to correspond.

3. No gear-case or other equipment that is not essential.

4. A reasonable use of bright fittings to make the machine look attractive.

5. Celluloid or aluminium mudguards, light in weight and of moderate width.

6. Light-weight wheels having narrow rims fitted with tyres of the " speed " type.

7. Light brakes of the calliper pattern.

8. Light front and rear lamps, easily removable, so that they need not be carried on summer excursions when the rider has no intention of staying out after dark.

9. No luggage-carrier, but possibly a light support for a saddle-bag.

10. A single fixed gear.

This machine is, of course, quite a sporty mount, although not actually a racing machine, and the owner will not treat it as a hack, but will be prepared to spend time and trouble keeping it in perfect condition.

Neither of the two machines we have just been discussing would be really suitable for all touring purposes.

The first, despite its three-speed gear, would be a hard machine to push for long distances in hilly country, because of its weight and the fact that the rider could not take up a really efficient riding position. The other machine would be inadequate in a different way. It would not be suitable for the carrying of a tourist's luggage. Nor would it be comfortable to ride on bad roads. And it would be tiring for long journeys in hilly country because of the lack of a variable gear.

What, then, are the characteristics of a good touring machine? They are:

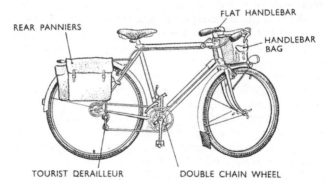

A Touring Bicycle

1. A comparatively low frame.
2. A flat or dropped handle-bar and a saddle of medium width, so that the rider can adopt a semi-racing or a cruising position at will and without discomfort.
3. No gear-case or other needless weight.
4. A reasonable use of plated parts.

5. Light-weight mudguards (celluloid or aluminium) of fairly wide section.

6. Well-built and substantial wheels with $1\frac{3}{8}$-inch rims, possibly fitted with tandem tyres having " semi-speed " treads.

7. Hub brakes or good substantial calliper brakes.

8. A light-weight dynamo lighting-system.

9. Adequate facilities for the carrying of luggage, well disposed between the front and the rear of the machine.

10 A multiple gearing system giving a range extending from the thirties to the eighties.

Very few people can afford to have three separate machines, each one designed to serve a particular purpose. The great majority of us have to be content with one, and in that case we naturally choose a model that can be fairly easily converted, when necessary, to serve one purpose or the other.

Quite obviously, a machine designed specially for utility riding, such as the one we first discussed, cannot be converted into the second type—the so-called club model—unless it is almost completely rebuilt. Those two machines do, in fact, represent the extremes so far as non-racing bicycles are concerned, and the touring machine may be regarded as something in between them.

A good touring machine is in many respects a compromise between the chief features of the light-weight club model and the heavier all-weather utility machine, with a few attributes of its own thrown in. If, therefore, a cyclist is proposing to draw up the specification for a bicycle that will have to serve him for all three purposes, he will designate something in the touring class. If, on the other hand, he is not so deeply interested in the acquisition of a machine resembling at all closely the ideal utility mount, he will specify something between the club model and the tourer.

Before anybody can draw up a complete specification

for a bicycle, he must study the various alternative components and accessories that can be combined to produce a bicycle of one kind or another. You yourself have now reached the stage in your cycling education where you can usefully examine the different parts of a bicycle. Above all, you want to know why there are in almost every case several alternatives, and for what particular purpose each of them is most suitable.

CHAPTER VII

CYCLE DESIGN—FRAME AND FORKS

THE foundation of a satisfactory bicycle specification is, of course, the frame itself, and now you have to consider such things as its shape and size, and the material from which it is made.

Whatever the size and whatever the shape of the frame you are going to choose, it must be strong enough for the job you expect it to do. In any case, however, strength does not necessarily imply weight.

Cyclists today are able to buy bicycles with frames made from metals that have been developed in the aeroplane-construction industry. Though those metals are themselves little, if any, lighter than the steels of which cycle frames used to be made a generation ago, they are of such remarkable strength that quite satisfactory frames can be produced from less actual metal.

The metal is made into tubes which have walls of almost incredible thinness. Nevertheless they are fully as strong as the thicker and heavier tubes made from other kinds of steel. The two best-known examples of the specially light tubes are the products of the Reynolds Tube Company Limited, known as " 531 ", and the Kromo range of articles made by Accles and Pollock Limited.

Frames constructed with these light-weight tubes are naturally rather more expensive than the heavier ordinary kind, but the saving in weight, and especially the resulting feeling of " liveliness ", are features for which the enthusiastic cyclist is willing to pay.

Where the question of expense has to be kept constantly in mind, it is generally better to buy a second-hand frame made from these special tubes rather than accept a new but heavier one. Nevertheless, the buying of second-hand frames is a risky undertaking unless the buyer has enough knowledge and experience to enable him to tell, by examination, whether the frame being offered for sale is in really good condition or has been damaged in some kind of accident. In particular, the prospective buyer should examine the various tubes near the lugs (especially the top and down tubes where they enter the steering-head), looking and feeling for " ripples " which may indicate distortion and weakening of the frame as a result of collisions.

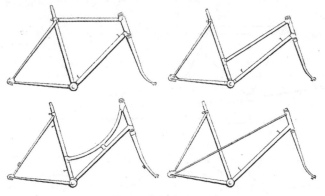

Types of Cycle Frame

There is not much variety in the shapes of bicycle frames. Almost all male and quite a number of female cycling enthusiasts use the standard " diamond ". A more usual shape for women and girls is, however, that in which the top tube of the diamond has been removed and an extra down tube incorporated. Frames of that kind have almost completely displaced the old-fashioned " loop " frame.

A third shape, originally introduced in France, is now beginning to make some headway in this country. Across the Channel it is generally known as the " cradle " or " mixed " frame, and its distinguishing feature is a

tube that goes from the top of the steering-head to join
the seat tube at a point above the bottom bracket,
and is then continued in a divided form to the rear
fork-end. In this country it has been variously named
as a " straight through " or " cross-over " frame.

Such a frame is not only well suited for use by women
and girls, but can equally reasonably be adopted by
male riders, although there is some natural prejudice
against it in that respect because it looks so much like
what is accepted as a woman's frame.

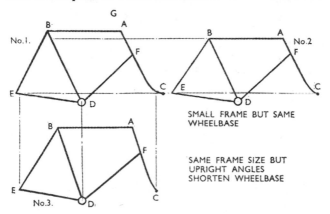

SMALL FRAME BUT SAME
WHEELBASE

SAME FRAME SIZE BUT
UPRIGHT ANGLES
SHORTEN WHEELBASE

Those are the three main types of cycle frame, but
quite considerable variations are possible in each case
without substantially altering the general shape. In
particular the length, height and " angle " of any given
type of frame may be adapted to suit some particular
purpose or to conform to the views of a particular school
of thought.

These possible variations are exemplified in an
exaggerated form in the drawings above.

Frame No. 1 is just as long as frame No. 2. That is
to say, the distance from C to E is the same in both
cases. The length of tube BD is, however, greater in
the case of frame No. 1. Frame No. 1 is therefore

technically a bigger frame because frame size is conventionally expressed as the length of the seat-tube, which is, of course, tube *BD*.

The measurement from *C* to *E* represents what is commonly described as the wheelbase. Strictly speaking, the wheelbase is the distance between the points at which the front and rear wheels touch the road, but obviously it is more convenient to measure it between the ends of the front and rear forks—that is to say, the points *C* and *E*. The most obvious difference

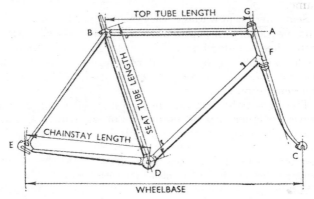

between No. 1 and No. 3 is that their wheelbases are not the same. Frame No. 3 is, in fact, noticeably shorter than No. 1.

So far as their actual size is concerned, measured in the conventional way, they are identical because tube *BD* is the same length in both instances. Nevertheless frame No. 3 is higher than frame No. 1. Moreover, the saddle position is further forward and more nearly over the bottom bracket (point *D*) because tube *BD* in frame No. 3 is more nearly vertical than the corresponding tube in frame No. 1. Similarly the top of the steering head (point *A*) is more nearly over the centre of the front wheel in the case of frame No. 3 than with frame No. 1.

Though, conventionally, frame No. 3 is the same size

as frame No. 1, there is in reality considerable difference between them. No. 3 is more " vertical " and more foreshortened than frame No. 1. The foreshortening is revealed by the wheelbase measurement—that is to say, the distance between points *C* and *E*. To express the " verticality " of the frame it is usual to give the measurement in degrees of angles *ABD* (known as the seat angle) and *GAB* (the head angle). They need not be the same, of course, though they often used to be, and when they are they give an appearance of " rightness " to the frame.

Seat angles nowadays vary between 68° and 73°. The most common is probably 70°, used in conjunction with a head angle of 70°. Not so long ago the popular angle was 68° or 69°. Modern cycles have, in fact, become noticeably more vertical or upright than those of a generation ago.

The bigger the seat and head angles of a frame, the nearer together will be points *C* and *E*, which are, of course, the front and rear fork-ends, in which the wheel-spindles are fitted. The more vertical the frame, therefore, the shorter the wheelbase, and the more forward the saddle and handle-bar positions.

Saddle and handle-bar positions can be varied, however, by the adoption of suitable stems. For example, the rider of a bicycle with a frame similar to No. 3 could, if he wished, adopt exactly the same saddle and handle-bar positions as those normally given by frame No. 1 merely by selecting saddle and handle-bar stems that would bring saddle and handle-bar grips farther back.

It will thus be seen that, though the seat and head angles of a cycle frame do affect saddle and handle-bar positions, the effect is not inevitable. There is, indeed, no reason why frame angles should be selected merely with the idea of achieving a particular saddle or handle-bar position. It must, however, be admitted that a fairly backward saddle position obtained by fitting a

backward-sweeping saddle stem to a very " upright "
cycle frame is not so comfortable as the same position
(relative to the bottom bracket) achieved by means of
a less vertical frame. The reason is that the rider of
the more vertical frame is in this case seated more
directly over the rear wheel.

Wheelbase

More important than the influence of frame angles
on saddle and handle-bar positions is their influence on
wheelbase. It is, in fact, very desirable that the prospective buyer of a bicycle should know in advance
exactly what he wants with regard to the length of the
wheelbase. He should certainly know—preferably from
experience—how a cycle with a short wheelbase differs
from one that is longer.

Although different riders may have rather different
ideas, it is generally true that a short wheelbase is an
advantage when riding up hills, a disadvantage when
riding fast down hills (especially if there are narrow
corners to be negotiated), and rather less easy to manage
than a long wheelbase in ordinary circumstances.

Anyone who has had experience of riding both
tandems and single bicycles will appreciate what an
effect differences of wheelbase can have on the control
of cycles and the ease with which they can be propelled
in different circumstances. Tandems are notoriously
sluggish up hills, but, on the other hand, the steersman
of a tandem usually has a feeling of confidence and
mastery which cannot be equalled when mounted on a
short-wheelbased machine.

There is a difference of something like 2 feet between
the wheelbase length of an ordinary single bicycle and
a normal tandem, but the difference between the
wheelbase of a very upright single cycle and one of
normal design is only a matter of 3 or 4 inches. Nevertheless, there are enthusiastic cyclists who assert that
the reduction of a cycle wheelbase from, say, 42 inches

ENQUIRING THE WAY.
Baylham . . SUFFOLK

to 40 inches makes all the difference in the world to its performance. The shorter wheelbase model is, they say, much livelier on hills, and in all circumstances the machine is more responsive to the rider's pedalling. The chief drawback is a greater tendency to skid on wet or slippery surfaces and increased difficulty in correcting a skid when it has started.

Taking everything into account, the most suitable wheelbase length for most riders and most circumstances will probably be round about 42 inches.

Earlier on we saw that the size of a bicycle frame is normally indicated by the length of the seat-tube (*BD* in the illustration). If all cycle frames had the same seat angles and were fitted with the same size of wheels, the length of the seat-tube would in itself be an adequate indication of the size of the resulting bicycle. In reality, however, the length of the seat-tube is not always a good enough guide to the practical size of a bicycle.

Before we can really appreciate the effective size of a bike we must know not only the size of the frame measured in the conventional way, but also its shape. Not only does an upright shape result in a higher bicycle than one with a frame having a smaller seat angle, but another important factor that has to be taken into account is the position of the bottom bracket.

The height of the bottom bracket above the ground has an important bearing on the height of the saddle, and consequently the rider's position. If, for example, a bicycle has a bottom bracket $12\frac{1}{2}$ inches above the ground, and another machine, with a frame of the same size, has its bracket 2 inches lower, obviously the rider of the first machine will be 2 inches higher than if he were mounted on the second one. The so-called " reach " will be the same in both cases, assuming that the seat-tubes and pedal-cranks are of the same length. In other words, the distance from the saddle to the pedal at its lowest point will be the same in the case of the machine with the high bottom bracket as in the other instance, but the rider of the machine with the lower bottom bracket will find it much easier to reach the ground with one foot when he halts.

That is quite an important point, especially for cyclists who ride in busy city streets, where it is a decided advantage to be able to pull up safely without having to dismount. Moreover, the lower the bottom bracket, the lower is the centre of gravity of machine and rider, with a consequent improvement in the rider's control over the machine in difficult circumstances. Wind resistance will also be slightly reduced.

The lowest practical height for a bottom bracket is $10\frac{1}{2}$ inches above the ground, assuming that the machine is fitted with cranks $6\frac{1}{2}$ inches long, which is the usual length nowadays. In such circumstances there is a margin of 4 inches to cover the projection of the front and side of the pedal at the lowest position.

Frame Size

So far as the frame is concerned, the only important point to be settled now is the size. We have to specify the length of seat-tube that will give us the machine we want, but before doing so we must decide whether we are normally going to ride with the saddle-stem projecting well above the seat-tube or merely protruding a little. A few years ago it was fashionable to use quite small cycle frames and have long saddle-stems, because it was said that the smaller frame was more rigid and lighter in weight, as it naturally contained less metal. Nowadays, however, there is less enthusiasm for very small frames, and most riders prefer to have the top of the saddle $2\frac{1}{2}$ or 3 inches above the top of the seat-tube.

Suppose, therefore, that the top of the saddle is going to be $2\frac{1}{2}$ inches above the top of the seat-tube, and that the pedal-cranks are to be the normal $6\frac{1}{2}$ inches in length. In that case the seat-tube must be at least 9 inches shorter than the rider's leg length. He will then just be able to reach the pedals when they are in the lowest position.

As we have assumed that the top of the saddle is going to be $2\frac{1}{2}$ inches above the top of the seat-tube, we have in fact decided that the saddle is going to be kept at its lowest position, because the saddle chassis and attachments will take up most of the $2\frac{1}{2}$-inch space. It would be better to decide to have the saddle a little higher, so that it can be raised or lowered if necessary. That means choosing a smaller frame than one having a seat-tube 9 inches shorter than the leg length. In general, therefore, it is advisable to select a frame size ten or eleven inches less than the length of the rider's leg from the crutch to the sole of the foot.

Fork Offset

Closely dependent on the design of the frame is the shape of the front fork to be fitted to it, and now we

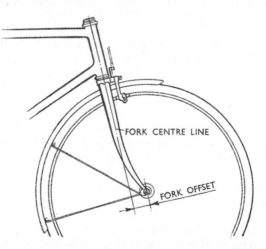

must have a look at a factor known as fork offset. From the drawing on this page it will be seen that the centre of the front wheel of a bicycle is not situated on the straight line represented by a continuation of the handle-bar stem towards the ground. It is in front of it, and the distance in front, measured at right angles to the line, represents the extent to which the fork-end is said to be offset.

This offsetting of the front wheel-spindle is an important factor in the design of a bicycle. It varies according to the head angle of the frame into which the fork is fitted. The steeper the angle, the less the amount of offset required to produce any given effect.

The smaller the amount of offset, the more readily will the wheel turn in any direction and the less will it resist changes of direction produced by movement of the handle-bar. With a greater amount of offset the wheel will show a more pronounced tendency to keep going in a straight line, but if the amount of offset is too great the wheel will tend to sway rhythmically from side to side.

From time to time various formulæ have been proposed for the calculation of fork offset, but they are of no real practical importance to the average cyclist, who can safely take as the basis of good fork design for ordinary purposes the following values :—

Head Angles	Offset
68°	2½ ins.
70°	2¼ ,,
72°	2 ,,

Those values are quite satisfactory for normal purposes, but they may be varied where it is desired to produce some special effect. Cycle-polo players, for instance, use bicycles that are fitted with straight forks, because the game demands that they should be able to turn instantaneously in any direction. Similarly, some tourists who habitually ride over bad roads adopt forks with slightly less offset than normal to increase the manœuvrability of their machines.

At the other end of the cycle frame, where the seat-

stays and the chain-stays meet, is the rear fork-end.
Like the end of the front fork, it is made to receive a
cycle wheel. Nowadays most rear fork-ends are designed
with a forward-facing opening, which makes it easier to
remove the wheel when necessary. When fork-ends of
that kind were first introduced they were, in fact,
generally described as " drop-outs ".

When a wheel is being removed from a fork-end of this
type, the chain does not offer any resistance to the
forward movement, but with the older type, in which
the openings face to the rear, the tendency of the chain
is to pull the wheel away from the opening. A feature of
the older pattern of fork-end was the inclusion of a chain-
adjuster. That was a little appliance fitting over the
spindle of the wheel and the fork-end itself, so that the
turning of small nuts caused the wheel to be forced
backwards, thus tightening the cycle chain, or allowed
it to move forward, and so slackened the chain. In
either case, of course, the ordinary nuts on the spindle
had first to be unscrewed and later tightened up again.

Chain-tensioning devices are not so important as
might be thought, except when derailleur gears are used,
in which case the device must be self-adjusting, and
usually takes the form of a small spring-controlled sprocket
that rides on the lower run of the chain, and so keeps
it taut. For normal purposes the tension can be
adjusted by moving the wheel backwards or forwards
in the slot of the rear fork-end.

One advantage of the old-fashioned chain-adjuster was
that it did prevent forward movement of the wheel as a
result of great pressure on the pedals, and recently some
of the racing cyclists have found it worth while adopting
a rather similar fitting for use with the modern type of
fork-end. Racing cyclists put much more pressure on
the pedals than do ordinary riders, and generally
speaking there is no reason at all why the average cyclist
should not be able to tighten the spindle-nuts enough to
keep his rear wheel fixed in the desired position.

CHAPTER VIII

CYCLE DESIGN—WHEELS AND TYRES

INTO the two fork-ends, as we have already seen, are fitted the wheels of the bicycle. Usually they are 26 inches in diameter (when measured with an inflated tyre in position). There are, however, quite a number of enthusiastic cyclists who prefer 27-inch wheels. That size has the effect of raising the height of the bicycle by half an inch as compared with the use of 26-inch wheels.

Advocates of the 27-inch wheel say that it is a little more lively and a little more comfortable than a similar wheel of the now normal 26-inch size. For many riders, however, the raising of the bottom bracket height by the extra half-inch is a disadvantage that outweighs any advantage there may be in the " rolling " of the wheel.

For tourists especially the disadvantages of a 27-inch wheel may be intolerable. Such riders often have to come to a halt without dismounting from their machines, heavily loaded with luggage. In those circumstances it is essential that the rider should be able to support machine and luggage by touching the ground with his toes.

Wheel Rims

The old-fashioned 28-inch wheel is now practically obsolete, and so are the $1\frac{1}{2}$-inch rims. Riders who value the extra comfort given by the old $1\frac{1}{2}$-inch tyre obtain it nowadays by using $1\frac{3}{8}$-inch rims fitted with the appropriate tandem tyres.

Rims $1\frac{3}{8}$ inches wide are now standard for touring and utility machines. Bicycles intended for more sporting purposes are normally fitted with $1\frac{1}{4}$-inch rims, and for racing purposes they may be reduced to $1\frac{1}{8}$ inches or even 1 inch.

It is quite obvious that the wider rims, being fitted with fatter tyres, will give a more pronounced cushioning effect. Equally obviously the area of tyre in contact with the road will be greater, and as a result the adhesion between tyre and road surface will be greater.

Riders have to choose for themselves whether they want the maximum comfort and the maximum hold on the road, or whether their chief interest is in speed and liveliness, in which case they will try to reduce the area of contact between tyre and road surface, and be prepared to pay for the reduction of " drag " by a corresponding reduction in comfort.

A cyclist to whom comfort is important will choose $1\frac{3}{8}$-inch rims in spite of the fact that they will be a little more sluggish than $1\frac{1}{4}$-inch rims. If, on the other hand, his chief concern is speed, he will certainly not choose anything fatter than $1\frac{1}{4}$ inches; in fact if he intends to do any serious racing, he will go in for sprint wheels and tubular tyres $1\frac{1}{8}$ inches wide, or possibly even narrower.

Although the increased friction produced by the use of wide tyres is an obstacle of some importance to the speedman, to the ordinary cyclist it may be an actual advantage in wet or slippery weather.

Cycle wheels, other than those designed purely for racing, are nowadays made of steel or aluminium alloy. Aluminium is dearer, but lighter. So far as shape is concerned, there are now three main patterns: first the old Westwood type, then the Endrick pattern, which superseded it for light-weight bicycles when calliper brakes began to be popular, and finally the up-to-date crescent shape of aluminium alloy rims.

The old-style Westwood rim was adopted in the days when brakes were of the pull-up type, acting on that part of the wheel rim nearest to the spoke-heads. Such a combination of brake and rim makes it difficult to remove the wheel quickly, and it was with the idea of facilitating quick wheel removal that the Endrick

(straight side) rims and calliper brakes were first introduced. The shape of aluminium alloy rims was not
determined by questions of braking or wheel removal,
but primarily to produce a sufficiently strong rim from a
material less robust than steel.

Spokes

The spokes of a cycle wheel are made of plated or
stainless steel (now by no means so rare as it was ten or
fifteen years ago). Stainless steel has obvious advantages for use in a part of the bicycle that is constantly in
contact with mud and moisture.

The thickness of the spokes is indicated by a scale of
" gauges ": the smaller the number of the gauge the
thicker the metal. There is, however, no method of
immediately converting gauge measurements into actual
thicknesses in terms of fractions of an inch.

Normally spokes of 15 gauge are fitted to a good
ordinary bicycle rear wheel, but of course a rider who
wishes to have a particularly strong wheel for " rough-
stuff " touring, or because he is himself an unusually
heavy rider, may specify a thicker gauge—say 14.
Additional strength can also be obtained by the use of
" butted " spokes, which are thicker at one or both ends.

Another method of increasing the strength of cycle
wheels, more popular a few years ago than it is now, is
to tie the spokes together with wire where they cross
one another and then solder the joints. An obvious
disadvantage of this procedure is that it makes it more
difficult to remove and replace a broken spoke. The
real reason why former advocates are not now so
enthusiastic is that it seemed to make the wheel rather
too rigid.

At one time it was quite common for the spokes in the
rear wheels of tandems fitted with hub gears and hub
brakes to snap off near the hub flange. That trouble is
not so common nowadays, though it is still by no means
unknown. A remedy is to have the wheels built with a

little washer at the point where each spoke passes
through the hub flange.

Just as there are several kinds of cycle-wheel rim,
each being designed to suit the requirements of a particular type of rider, so there are different kinds of tyres
for fitting to cycle wheels. There is greater variety of
choice in the case of tyres than with regard to rims.
Generally speaking, however, cycle tyres may be roughly
divided into four main classes.

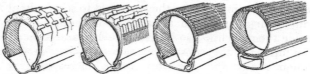

WESTWOOD RIM   WESTRICK RIM &   ENDRICK RIM &   SPRINT RIM &
& ROADSTER   TOURING TYRE   SPEED TYRE   TUBULAR RACING
TYRE   TYRE

At one end of the scale is the roadster type, which
has the heaviest tread of all. It is intended for use on
the kind of bicycle designed for utility purposes, and
its chief characteristic is the rugged pattern of rubber
" feet ", which give it a firm grip on the road surface.
Tyres of this kind are designed to give the maximum
safety and comfort; they are not intended to be fast.

At the other extreme is the type of tyre designed
primarily for speed. Known as a tubular, it is little
more than an air-tube to which a very light tread has
been added. Tubulars differ from all other cycle tyres
in having no separate outer cover. They are themselves
a combination of air-tube and cover, in which the cover
has been reduced to the absolute minimum.

Special rims are needed for use with tubulars, and the
tyres are kept in position either by air pressure alone
or by air pressure assisted by some kind of adhesive.
The sides or walls of a tubular tyre are not entirely
naked, but are usually covered by a layer of cotton
threads so arranged that the tube proper can be pulled

through the protective covering when necessary for repairs.

Tubular repairs are more difficult to carry out than in the case of ordinary tyres consisting of tubes and separate covers. It is therefore normal practice for users of tubular tyres to carry spares and replace a punctured tyre with a new one, so that the actual repair can be made later.

Although tubular tyres are produced principally for racing purposes, and are considerably more expensive than ordinary tyres, they are used to some extent for club riding, and even for touring by enthusiasts who value their liveliness so highly that they are prepared to put up with the consequent reduction in comfort on rough roads and the very much increased risk of puncturing.

Tubular tyres are used with the narrowest of rims, made in the appropriate double-concave form, whereas roadster tyres are normally produced only in the wider sizes.

More generally suitable for club riding and week-end excursions are the types of tyre included in what is commonly called the speed group. They have treads which offer little resistance to forward movement, though they are slightly heavier than tubulars, and are intended to be both fast and lively without the risk of puncturing which is inseparable from the use of tubulars.

Usually the tread of speed tyres consists of a series of narrow ribs running in the direction of travel, and there are no knobs or blocks of rubber, such as those which form the characteristic pattern of roadster tyres. There is, however, a type of tyre which may be regarded as a compromise between the speed and the roadster types. It is the tourist tyre, and embodies some of the ruggedness of the roadster tread with the more lively ribbing of the speed type.

Both the tourist and speed type of tyre are obtainable in the $1\frac{1}{4}$- and $1\frac{3}{8}$-inch rim sizes. They may also be had in the tandem form, which is really an oversize tyre for use with any particular rim, and it is quite common for cyclists to use normal speed tyres on their machines for club riding and week-end excursions, but to substitute tandem tyres of the tourist pattern before setting off for holiday tours.

Two kinds of valve are used for the inflation of modern tyres. One is the long-established Woods type, in which a small rubber sleeve is used to cover a hole in a metal tube through which the air is forced from the pump into the air-tube. Air enters under pressure, and so reaches the air-tube, but it cannot return because the internal pressure causes the rubber sleeve to seal the hole in the metal tube. This type of valve is quite satisfactory so long as the rubber is not allowed to perish and is changed when necessary.

A more modern type of valve is fitted to the lightest kind of tyre. Although there is more than one pattern, they are all basically the same—a kind of needle-valve, working on the principle that the ingoing air has to force the valve from its seating, and when the inflation pressure ceases, the pressure of air in the tube itself effectively closes the valve.

With valves of the needle type it is easier to pump up a tyre, and if the dust-cap is always replaced after inflation, they will work without trouble for as long as is necessary. A few grains of dust on the valve seating will, however, inevitably cause the valve to leak.

CHAPTER IX

CYCLE DESIGN—GEARING, DRIVE AND BRAKES

You already know that the gear of a bicycle depends on the relative sizes of the chainwheel, the rear sprocket and the rear wheel. You know, too, that it may be altered by changing any of those three factors.

It is, however, seldom practicable to change a rear wheel and replace it with another of different size. In practice the gear of a single-speed bicycle is normally changed by the substitution of a different rear sprocket or possibly another chainwheel. Modern chainwheels are often fitted with detachable " rings " (the outer parts which carry the actual teeth), and by substituting another ring with more or fewer teeth it is possible to vary the gearing. A cheaper method is to unscrew the rear sprocket and put in its place another of different size.

Those methods are practicable when it is desired to change the gear of a bicycle permanently. For temporary or momentary changes they are quite out of the question. No rider could be expected to change a chain ring or a rear sprocket during the course of a ride ; yet it is often desirable to change gear during a ride, especially in hilly country. In such cases it is obviously an advantage to have a bicycle fitted with more than one rear sprocket or more than one chain ring and some arrangement for transferring the chain from one to the other. In that way the rider can change chainwheel or rear sprocket without actually having to remove and replace them.

Derailleur Gearing

This method of gear-changing by derailment was largely developed in France, where it is now quite normal for all types of bicycle. The method has been adopted to a great extent in Britain for club models and touring machines, but is seldom used with the utility type, for which the hub gear (to be discussed later) is still the favourite.

Nowadays it is possible to have derailleur-gear equipment comprising a chainwheel with as many as

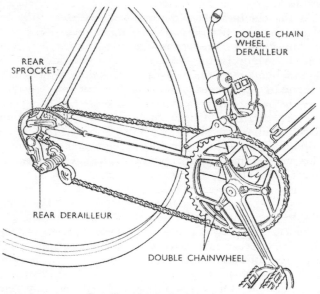

REAR SPROCKET

DOUBLE CHAIN WHEEL DERAILLEUR

REAR DERAILLEUR

DOUBLE CHAINWHEEL

Derailleur Method of Gearing

three rings of teeth and a rear sprocket block containing up to five sprockets. As the chain can be made to run on any of the chain rings and any of the sprockets, there are in such a case theoretically fifteen different gear ratios available.

In practice, however, the effective number is smaller because of overlapping of the resultant gear ratios and the fact that it is rarely possible to run the chain satisfactorily from the innermost chainwheel ring to the outermost sprocket.

With derailleur gears the chain is frequently running out of alignment, and there is no doubt that it will wear out more quickly than if used on a single-geared machine with chainwheel and sprocket in perfect alignment. The reduction in life is, however, not very serious.

As the chainwheels and sprockets used in derailleur gears are of varying sizes, the length of chain required to connect them is not constant. It is therefore necessary to include in the derailing mechanism some kind of tensioning device that will take up the slack chain when it is running on the smaller sprockets and rings.

With the derailleur type of gear mechanism the rider has great freedom in the choice of ratios, as he can fit sprockets of whatever sizes he likes and combine them with chain rings according to his particular fancies. The mechanism is moreover always open to inspection and comparatively simple to repair if anything goes wrong.

Hub Gears

The traditional type of variable gear mechanism in this country is the two-, three- or four-speed hub gear. It consists of an enlarged rear hub in which there is a special assembly of cogs to transmit the drive from the spindle of the wheel to the wheel itself. By the movement of the control cable the cogs can be moved laterally and made to form varying combinations. In that way the number of revolutions made by the rear wheel can be varied in relation to the number made by the sprocket. With the original standard three-speed hub, for example, when the control lever is in the "normal" position the rear wheel and the rear sprocket revolve at the same speed. They do, in fact, make one solid unit. If, however, the control lever is moved to the high-gear position, the rear wheel will revolve one and a third times for every revolution of the sprocket, and in the low-gear position it will make only three-quarters of a revolution each time the rear sprocket completes a full turn.

The standard three-speed is not by any means the only type of hub gear available. There are in fact two-, three- and four-speed hubs with wide, medium and close ratios. With the wide-ratio gears the high and low gears are as far apart as possible, and of course the

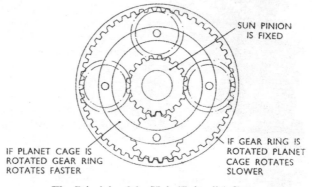

SUN PINION
IS FIXED

IF PLANET CAGE IS
ROTATED GEAR RING
ROTATES FASTER

IF GEAR RING IS
ROTATED PLANET
CAGE ROTATES
SLOWER

The Principle of the Hub (Epicyclic) Gear

close ratios offer variability of gearing over a much narrower range.

Hub gears may be combined with derailleur gears. If, for instance, a double rear sprocket and derailleur mechanism is combined with a standard three-speed hub, the rider will have six gears available for use—three for each of the two sprockets.

Similarly a triple derailleur and a three-speed hub would give nine gears. It is, however, difficult to devise a combination of derailleur and hub gear that will give a satisfactory range of ratios without overlapping. Two interesting combinations worth mentioning are the following (for 26-inch wheels) :—

BOSSINGTON...EXMOOR.

Derailleur sprockets	Chainwheel	Gears produced with standard 3-speed hub
19 } 22 }	46	{ 40·6, 47·2 54·4, 62·9 72·5, 83·8
18 } 21 }	36	{ 33·5, 39, 44·5 52, 59·4, 69

Attached to the chainwheel of a bicycle are the cranks and pedals. Cranks are nowadays standardised at 6½ inches long for adult riders, but it is still possible for tall men to obtain them 7 inches long, thus gaining a little extra leverage, which may help them to propel a

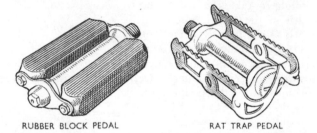

RUBBER BLOCK PEDAL   RAT TRAP PEDAL

slightly higher gear. With the longer cranks it is, of course, necessary to have a bottom bracket half an inch higher than usual, in order to give the necessary clearance between pedals and the ground.

Pedals may be made entirely of metal (rat traps) or incorporate blocks of rubber. Those are the two main types, although nowadays it is possible to buy pedals that combine the features of both the original patterns.

Rat-trap pedals are lighter than those using rubber blocks, and they give a better grip for the shoes, especially when used in wet weather, but they are not so comfortable with light footwear. For comfort the rubber-block type of pedal is rather better than the rat trap, but it is heavier, and in wet weather it lets the foot slide about. Rubber pedals do not, in fact, give so sure a grip as do rat traps, and for that reason they are less suitable for strong pedalling and do not help the rider to develop a good pedalling style.

Rubber blocks wear out much more quickly than the teeth of rat-trap pedals, and at intervals they have to be renewed; but that is not a costly business.

Rat-trap pedals make rows of teeth-marks on the soles of shoes, but that again is not a serious matter, and there is no need to think that any real damage is done to the footwear.

Whatever kind of pedal is used—whether rat trap or rubber, or some combination of the two—it surely ought to be obvious that the type chosen should be wide enough to take the rider's foot. In other words, the width of the pedal should be at least as great as the width of the broad part of the rider's shoe. Nevertheless it is by no means unusual for cycle-makers to fit their light-weight club-model bicycles with pedals that are absurdly narrow. There are, indeed, makers who normally put wider pedals on their juvenile bicycles than they do on some of the machines they intend to be used by adults. So when you buy a new bicycle see that the pedal is wide enough to take the kind of shoe you are going to wear when riding it, and do not forget that if you are going touring you will probably want to wear quite substantial shoes, so that you can also include a bit of rough-stuff walking without hurting your feet.

It is quite common for users of rat-trap pedals to equip them with toe-straps or clips to prevent the feet from moving too far forward and to help to some extent in the upward movement of pedalling. When buying toe-clips and the kind of toe-strap that is combined with a clip, you should make sure that they are exactly the right size and that they will allow the toe of your shoe to project over the front of the pedal far enough for the broad part of your foot to be placed over the pedal spindle. If they do not allow your foot to take up a position far enough forward, you will find that pedalling

with your toes can become very painful. On the other
hand, the clips should not allow your toes to go so far

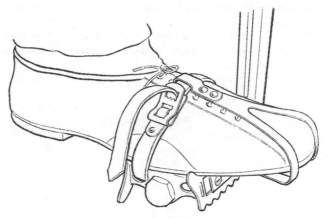

Toe-clip and Strap

forward that the narrow part of the foot is on the actual
pedals.

Brakes

Although your main interest is to equip your bicycle
with the means for making it go as easily as possible,
you must not overlook the need to be able to bring it
to a standstill smoothly and safely when necessary. In
modern conditions the brakes of a bicycle are, indeed,
a very important part of its equipment.

The commonest type of cycle brake is that in which
the retarding force is applied to the rim of the wheel.
It exists in several forms. The oldest—now fitted only
to roadster machines or children's bicycles having
Westwood rims—is the pull-up or stirrup pattern. At
the open end of the " stirrup " are two brake-blocks
made of rubber or composition which, when the brake-
lever is operated, are brought into contact with that part

of the wheel rim nearest the spokes. Usually the operating lever is of the roller type, held in position by means
of metal eyelets on the handle-bar, and the effort is
transmitted to the actual brake by means of a series of
metal rods.

Brakes of that kind are very efficient so long as they
are maintained in good working order. There is,

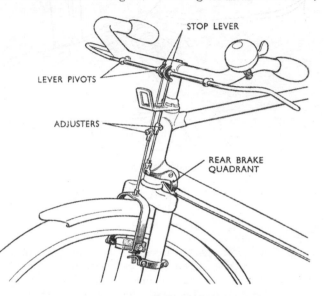

Stirrup Brake Mechanism

however, a tendency for the lever-and-rod transmission
system to rattle when the machine is ridden over rough
roads. A more serious defect is the fact that stirrup
brakes prevent the easy removal of the wheel.

It was to facilitate wheel-removal that the calliper
pattern of rim brake was introduced. In this case the
brake-blocks do not come into contact with the inner
surface of the wheel rim, but operate on the sides of a

specially shaped rim (Endrick) having vertical sides of greater depth than is usual with the original Westwood rims.

In its most modern form the calliper brake (or, to give it the name which now seems more appropriate, the cantilever brake) is not only efficient, but also very simple in construction. The two brake-blocks are connected by means of a wire or other flexible link which passes

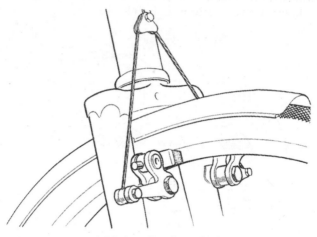

A Modern Cantilever Brake

over a small pulley or rocker bar, to which the actual brake-cable is attached. Thus, when the brake-lever is operated and the brake-cable is pulled, the power is transmitted to both brake-blocks irrespective of any unevenness that there may be in the wheel rim. Such brakes are said to be compensated in action, and they have obvious advantages over other patterns in which the braking efficiency is reduced by unevennesses in the wheel rim.

All forms of rim brake become inefficient when the rim is wet, and on rainy days the rider of a bicycle so equipped must always remember that, when he applies his brakes, there will be an interval during which they will have no retarding effect. Only when, by friction, they have removed the moisture from the rim will they bring the bicycle to a standstill.

That defect is obviously inseparable from the use of brake-blocks operating on the wheel rims, but it does not exist in the case of the second main type of cycle brake—hub brakes.

There are two patterns of hub brake, but the principle

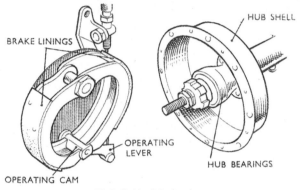

Hub Brake Mechanism

is the same in both instances. Both produce their retarding effect by friction on the inside of the hub of the wheel or a specially enlarged part of it (the drum). Drum brakes may be either cable-operated or rod-operated or (usually in the case of tandems) a combination of both. Where, however, the whole of the inside of the hub (without enlargement) is used, the brake is operated by backwards pressure on the pedals —i.e. through the anti-clockwise turning of the rear sprocket. The latter type of brake is known as the coaster or back-pedalling hub. It is much less popular in this country than on the Continent, though, like the drum brake, it can be usefully combined with a variable-gear hub.

Hub brakes, being completely enclosed, are unaffected by rain or snow, but care must be taken to prevent the entry of oil between the brake linings and the inner surface of the drum or hub. If oil does get on to the linings it immediately renders the brake useless, and its removal is always a very troublesome business.

Although some cycle tourists have a special affection for hub brakes, their use is mainly confined to tandems, and in those cases it is not unusual for the two hub brakes to be supplemented by a rim brake acting on the rear wheel.

CHAPTER X

CYCLE DESIGN—HANDLE-BARS AND SADDLES

IF you are not an experienced cyclist it is almost certain that you have some degree of antipathy to what are known as dropped handle-bars. You may believe that they restrict the rider's chest and induce curvature of the spine. In any case, you are almost certain to regard them as dangerous on the grounds that they make it difficult, if not impossible, for the rider to see where he is going.

Unfortunately some young and misguided cyclists give apparent support to those impressions by using dropped handle-bars fixed in the lowest possible position, in conjunction with saddles raised as high as they can possibly tolerate. Those youngsters are no doubt inspired by the achievements of famous racing cyclists, but the riding positions which they themselves attain are not really akin to those of their heroes. In any case, a position which is suitable for a cyclist on a racing track, interested only in getting the maximum speed out of himself and his machine, is not altogether appropriate for a boy who merely uses his bicycle to ride between home and school and has to share the roads with other forms of traffic.

A bicycle handle-bar must be judged by the positions it makes available to an intelligent rider, and not by the position which some misguided child may adopt. Usually it matters little whether the handle-bar is upturned or not, because the up-and-down adjustment of the stem makes it possible for the grips to be brought into the desired position merely by raising or lowering the bar as a whole. In the diagrams on page 20, for instance, the position of the rider's hands is identical in all cases, although one bar is nominally raised, another is dropped and one is flat. It would be absurd to condemn the so-called dropped bar merely for its shape.

If a rider is satisfied with one position for his hands, day in and day out, uphill and down, when he is taking things easily or when he is in a hurry, then it is entirely a matter of taste as to whether he chooses the first or the second shape of handle-bar. Most riders, however, cannot manage in all circumstances with one set position for their hands, any more than they can manage with one gear for all circumstances. If they adopt a bar of the standard upturned pattern, such as is generally fitted to the old-fashioned roadster bicycle, it is almost certain that when the going is hard—when climbing a hill or fighting a head wind—they will automatically try to obtain a more efficient position by grasping the centre of the bar because it is lower and further forward than the normal hand position.

The chief disadvantage of the old-fashioned upturned handle-bar is, in fact, that the grips are too far back and there is no satisfactory alternative position for use in difficult circumstances. With a dropped handle-bar, however, the rider has the choice of at least two alternative positions—on the " drops " and on the upper part of the handle-bar. Even if he is content to adopt one position for all circumstances, he will still be better suited with a dropped handle-bar than with the standard upturned bar, not because of the actual drop, but by reason of the forward extension of the bar.

The standard upturned bar sweeps backwards, whereas all forms of dropped handle-bar carry the rider's hands forward rather than backwards. That is their main advantage. It is practically impossible for any cyclist of normal build to find an efficient riding position if his hands are behind the handle-bar stem.

There is less danger of constriction of the chest with a dropped handle-bar than there is with a standard upturned handle-bar because, if the rider of a machine with a dropped handle-bar does take hold of the centre part of the bar, he does so when " cruising " with his arms limp, whereas when the rider with a standard up-turned bar grasps the centre portion he is usually ex-erting himself to the utmost, and is, in fact, seriously handicapped by the hand position he is forced to adopt in his efforts to make the best use of his energy.

A dropped handle-bar, of adequate width (which means no less wide than the rider's shoulders), intelligently adjusted, not only gives the rider an efficient position, but actually helps him to breathe deeply without any fear of constriction of the chest.

Saddles

So far as comfort is concerned the saddle of a bicycle is probably its most important component. Yet a regrettably large proportion of the people who ride bicycles " make do " with saddles that are not at all suited to their requirements, although there are so many shapes and sizes available that nobody need put up with one that is not exactly right.

Many riders, especially when mounted on new machines, cheerfully accept discomfort as inevitable, under the impression that they must " break in " the saddle and suffer during the breaking-in process. There is no justification at all for such a belief. If a saddle is of the right kind for the rider and the kind of riding he is going to do, it should be comfortable from the very beginning. Far too many riders accept without question saddles of a type that are neither suited to their own build nor appropriate to their kind of riding.

Obviously, a very heavy rider needs a saddle that is not only strong enough to bear his weight but also sufficiently well sprung to absorb most of the ordinary road shocks. What is suitable for such a rider would not be suitable for someone of slight build, even assuming that they both practise the same kind of cycling (utility riding, touring or club riding for instance).

The suspension or springing of a saddle is quite an important feature in itself, and mistakes made in the choice of a saddle from that point of view can have unfortunate consequences, but equally important are the shape and size of the saddle. In that respect the deciding factor is not the weight of the rider, but the position he is going to adopt on the saddle, which in turn depends on the kind of cycling he is going to practise.

The utility rider, who makes only short journeys and normally sits bolt upright on the saddle in what we have previously described as the policeman's posture, uses his

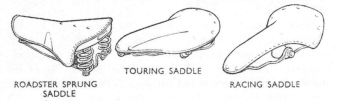

ROADSTER SPRUNG
SADDLE

TOURING SADDLE

RACING SADDLE

Three Main Types of Saddle

saddle as a real seat. He sits on it in the same way as he would sit on a high-backed chair or bench. The part of his pelvis which comes into contact with the saddle is the widest part, and consequently, if the saddle is to support him without discomfort, it should be at least as wide as that part of his anatomy.

If, however, the same rider leans forward so that his trunk makes an angle of about 45° with the vertical, his weight is no longer carried on the widest part of his pelvis. The bones which now come into contact with the saddle are not so widely spaced, and there is not the same necessity for a wide saddle. A wide saddle is, in fact, a disadvantage now because, in the forward inclined position which the rider has adopted, it will interfere with the free movement of the thighs, causing friction and chafing.

In this riding position the cyclist supports part of the weight of his upper body by leaning on the handle-bar, and it is not necessary for him to have such a well-sprung saddle as if he were sitting upright on it.

When the body is leaned still further forward, in the racing attitude, even less body-weight is carried by the saddle, so that the suspension can be reduced to a minimum. It is also still more necessary to make sure that the saddle does not obstruct movement of the thighs. That is why racing-saddles are very narrow, very hard and almost devoid of springing.

Between the two extremes of the narrow, almost unsprung, racing-saddle and the wide kind of seat with a very resilient suspension system, there are many different kinds. They vary in length, breadth, weight and springing (suspension). The rider can, in fact, select what he wishes between luxurious " arm-chair comfort " and austere efficiency (from the racing man's point of view) which is not uncomfortable when used for the purpose for which it is designed.

As a rule, older people tend to choose saddles that are too luxurious and often too wide, whereas young riders have a fondness for narrow saddles that are not suitable for the kind of riding which they practise.

The only safe rule to adopt when choosing a saddle is: select one that is wide enough and yet gives enough freedom for the legs and is resilient enough to carry the rider's weight in comfort without wasting efficiency through excessive " give ". In other words, the choice must depend on the build of the rider, the position he adopts on his bicycle, and the kind of cycling he intends to do.

CHAPTER XI

CYCLE DESIGN—LIGHTING AND LUGGAGE-CARRYING

IF you use a bicycle on a public road during the hours of darkness you must see that it is fitted with lamps giving a white front light and a red rear light. Perhaps by the time this book is published it will also be necessary for you to carry on your bicycle a red reflector and a white surface (see page 36).

For town riding it may be justifiable to use lamps that are just sufficient to comply with the law and not particularly bright, provided, of course, that all your riding is done in conditions where the street lighting makes both you and your machine completely visible to other road-users. Out in the open country, however, where street lamps are rare and often not very efficient, you need lights that are beyond reproach. Your front lamp especially should be good enough to illuminate the road ahead for a sufficient distance, so that, whatever may be your riding speed at the time, you can be sure of your ability to stop within the range of your head lamp.

Unfortunately none of the modern cycle lighting-systems is completely satisfactory. You must therefore choose the one that most appeals to you, and then take appropriate steps to guard against foreseeable failures.

Battery Lamps

Electric lamps of one kind or another are by far the most popular nowadays. In their cheapest and simplest form they are little more than metal containers for a dry battery and a bulb of appropriate size. When new they may seem to work satisfactorily, but before very long, if they are used during wet weather, they will give trouble.

The electrical contacts between battery and bulb, provided by the lamp-body itself, will deteriorate, causing difficulty in maintaining a continuous light and probably leading, in the end, to complete failure of the lamp.

Another defect of cheap battery lamps is that they soon begin to rattle—a source of irritation to any cyclist who takes a pride in his equipment, although it may have no detrimental effect on the lighting efficiency (unless, of course, the bulb itself begins to work loose in its flimsy holder).

There are some types of battery lamp which are free from these criticisms, beautifully made and robust, with electrical contacts not depending on the solidity and cleanliness of the lamp-body, but assured by the use of internal insulated wires. Such lamps, because of the quality of the reflectors embodied in them, make the best possible use of the light-source, but they are inevitably heavy.

Whatever kind of battery lamp is used, the battery eventually becomes exhausted (sometimes surprisingly quickly) and has to be replaced. The cost of the batteries can be quite an important item in the expenditure of a cyclist who makes good use of his bicycle during the winter months, as for instance riding appreciable distances to and from work. In such cases a dynamo lighting-set is more economical.

Dynamo Lighting

Recent improvements in the design of generators and lamps have made it possible for manufacturers of dynamo lighting-sets to say truthfully that they give an adequate light even when the speed of the bicycle falls to a walking pace. At greater speeds the light is more brilliant, and all lighting sets made by the well-known manufacturers provide quite a good light at normal cycling speeds. The faster the speed the greater the light, but in some cases safety devices are included in the design of the generator to prevent the output from becoming so great at high speeds that the bulbs will burn out.

The failure of bulbs owing to " burning out " is less common nowadays than it was a few years ago. Nevertheless, unless the rider makes sure that the bulbs he is using are of good quality and the type for which the lighting set was designed, the life of the bulbs may be surprisingly short.

Electrical overloading is not the only cause of bulb failure. Continual vibration and jolting may also result in the eventual breaking of the filaments, although it must be said that the filaments of the bulbs made by the well-known makers are nowadays remarkably durable.

Whatever form of electric lighting is used, it is obviously necessary for the rider to carry spares—bulbs and/or batteries.

Although there is no doubt that, for reasonably long journeys in the dark, the best kind of cycle lighting is that provided by acetylene gas lamps, they are now very rarely used except by a minority of enthusiastic riders who are prepared to give them the care and attention essential for their proper working. Most cyclists find acetylene lamps troublesome and inconvenient.

When you have decided for yourself what kind of cycle lighting you are going to adopt, you will have to make up your mind where you are going to fit the lamps. So far as the rear lamp is concerned there is not a great deal of choice : if the lamp is of the battery type it will be carried on a bracket on the right-hand seat-stay, or perhaps the hub spindle. The lighter lamps used in connection with dynamo sets, which are little more than bulb-holders, can be attached to almost any part of the bicycle, so long as it provides a good electrical contact (most dynamo lighting-sets use the cycle frame as part of the circuit between generator and lamps).

A rear light on the right-hand seat-stay is not always fully visible to traffic approaching from the left (as, for

instance, when the cyclist is riding over a cross-roads).
For that reason it is generally better to put the rear lamp
in a more obvious position, but it must not be on the
left-hand side of the machine.   Tourists whose machines
are fitted with luggage-carriers often attach the rear
light at the end of the carrier, or perhaps on the mudguard
itself, so that they may, when desired, put pannier bags
over the rear wheel without hiding the lamp.

So far as the front lamp is concerned, there is much
greater choice.   Members of cycling clubs and cycle

Three Possible Points of Attachment for the Front Lamp

tourists usually carry it on a bracket attached to the
offside front fork.   On the other hand, riders whose
use of the bicycle is purely utilitarian generally fit their
front lamps to a bracket at the top of the steering-head.
Neither position is really satisfactory.

Of the two, from the club-riding cyclist's point of view
the front-fork position is preferable, because it does not
interfere with his use of a cycling cape (which covers not
only the rider but the handle-bar as well).   In that
position, though, the lamp glass soon gets covered with
mud during bad weather, and unless the bracket is
securely fixed to the fork-blade there is always a risk that
some day it will slide down and cause an accident.

The utility rider probably does not wear a cape, and so may be quite content with a lamp fixed just in front of his handle-bar stem. When he is riding in lighted streets he is not dependent on his own lamp to illuminate the road ahead of him, and it does not matter whether it is fixed high or low on the machine. If, however, he rides regularly in unlighted country lanes he will find that the handle-bar position is rather too high to give adequate illumination.

Between those two extreme positions there is not at present in this country any generally available alternative. It seems very likely, however, that British cycle manufacturers will eventually follow Continental fashion and equip some of their machines at least with lamp-brackets fixed to the fork-head or to the front of small luggage-carriers over the front wheel. It will then be possible for the riders to use cycle capes during bad weather without disadvantage, because the capes will fit behind the lamps and in front of the handle-bar.

Luggage-carrying

The amount of luggage to be carried on a bicycle may be anything from a few simple tools and a repair outfit to the voluminous equipment of the ardent cycle-camping photographer. In any case, the machine should be equipped for carrying whatever its rider may need, and the load should interfere as little as possible with his control of the cycle.

The butterfly rider, who ventures out only when the sun is shining in a blue sky, need not encumber himself with the carrying of a cape or other protection against wet weather. His kit is so small that it does not matter whether he puts it in his pocket or in one of the old-fashioned tool-bags that are still to be seen suspended from the saddles of some roadster-type bicycles.

A more serious rider will always carry on his machine not only the necessary tools and repair outfit, but also a cape, and when he is going out for a whole day's ride he may take with him sandwiches, and perhaps, a thermos flask. Such a rider's requirements are quite adequately met by one of the popular types of saddle-bag.

A bag of that kind will probably be quite big enough to take the rider's luggage when he goes off for a week-end tour. In that case, however, it will be advisable to use a bag support, which is easily fitted to the seat-stays above the mudguard, to take some of the strain that otherwise would fall on the straps of the saddle-bag, and to keep the weight off the mudguard (especially if it is made of celluloid).

Even for extended tours lasting a couple of weeks, some

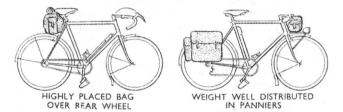

HIGHLY PLACED BAG   WEIGHT WELL DISTRIBUTED
OVER REAR WHEEL   IN PANNIERS

riders can get all their kit into one of the bigger saddle-bags. Most tourists find, though, that one bag is not enough for a long holiday. Some of them therefore fix another of the same kind, but perhaps not so wide, in front of the handle-bar. Others prefer to use panniers slung over the rear wheel, either in conjunction with a saddle-bag or instead of it.

If much luggage has to be carried on a bicycle it is best to fix it as low as possible and to avoid putting all the weight on the back wheel. The front wheel cannot carry so much weight as the back one, because of the effect on the steering, but if the weight is attached in such a way that it moves with the steering and does not wobble about, quite appreciable loads can be carried at the front, especially if they are placed low down—as, for instance, by the use of small panniers suspended from a suitable carrier fixed on the front fork.

If too much weight is added to the back wheel, which already bears the bulk of the rider's weight, the stability of the machine may be upset, especially when cornering or when the loaded bicycle is being wheeled.

In this country it is usual to fasten luggage to the bicycle by means of straps, but a more convenient method is used on the Continent. There thick elastic cords with metal hooks at each end are used. They make it possible to attach ungainly and cumbersome parcels to a cycle carrier, and are easier to manipulate than the straps and buckles to which we are accustomed.

CHAPTER XII

LOOKING AFTER THE BICYCLE

EVERYBODY who owns a good bicycle ought at least to try to keep it in good condition. Most of them do indeed start off with a determination to maintain it in the glistening state in which it was delivered to them by the maker or dealer, and many of them go so far as to spend a few minutes cleaning the machine after each day's use, especially if the weather has been bad. Before long, however, their enthusiasm for the job begins to wane; the cleanings become less and less frequent, and the bicycle begins to look more and more obviously second-hand.

That is a pity, but not so regrettable as the fact that even more cyclists, owners of good machines, fail to keep them in sound mechanical condition. A bicycle may be brilliantly polished and completely free from dust and dirt, and yet in poor condition mechanically as a result of neglect. Similarly, a cycle that is perfectly sound mechanically may look shabby and unattractive because its owner is more interested in mechanical efficiency than in the appearance of his machine, although generally speaking the rider who takes a pride in the mechanical perfection of his mount will not neglect its appearance.

A bicycle is not a complicated piece of machinery, and every owner of one who is no longer a school child should be able to keep it in good running order. No profound mechanical knowledge is required, and it is not suggested that the average cyclist should undertake cycle repairing. When that becomes necessary he will be well advised to put the job into the hands of a qualified man. But by undertaking the regular examination and maintenance of his cycle he will certainly make it less

likely for him to have to take a major repair job to a
professional cycle mechanic.

Routine Inspection

The cyclist who treats a good cycle with the care
that it deserves does not limit his attention to examina-
tions at any given interval: he is constantly inspecting
it. When he takes it out of the cycle shed he automatically runs his eye over it, tests the inflation of his
tyres, perhaps fingers the brake-levers to see that they
are still well adjusted and working satisfactorily, and
almost without knowing it checks other components and
accessories. He cannot just take the bicycle and ride it
without giving any thought to it.

Out on the road, too, he does not forget the cycle,
even though he may not be fully conscious of the fact
that he is taking care of it. If there is something slightly
out of order, he knows at once. If the cycle is not
running silently, he is immediately aware of the clicking
or the squeaking or the rattling that has developed, and
his immediate concern is to locate it and cure it.

First of all, he stops pedalling. If the noise stops too,
he is fairly certain that it came from some item in the
transmission—it may be the chain, the chainwheel, a
crank, a pedal—or it *may* be the saddle that is squeaking
only when the rider's legs move. If when pedalling is
resumed the noise is found to occur once with every
revolution of the pedals, then the possible cause is still
further limited. If, on the other hand, the noise is
repeated at regular intervals but less frequently than
once for each turn of the cranks, the chain will be
suspected.

In that way the conscientious rider gets to the bottom
of every unusual (and therefore unwanted) sound,
locating its origin, so that it may be remedied. Of
course, it is not always easy to identify and locate an
unwanted noise—some can be quite baffling, as, for
instance, the sounds sometimes produced by cotter-pins

that have worked slightly loose, but not loose enough for the rider to feel the play when pedalling. But whatever the cause, the rider who takes a pride in his cycling and his cycle will not be satisfied until he has restored his machine to its normal silky silence.

Not only does such a rider keep his ears open all the time, but he is also constantly noticing the " feel " of his mount. If, for example, the nuts that fasten the rear wheel in the fork-ends have not been tightened up enough, with the result that pressure on the pedals, transmitted through the chain, has pulled the sprocket side of the wheel slightly forward, the rider may not be immediately conscious of the fact that his wheel is slightly askew, but as soon as there is the slightest rubbing against one of the brake-blocks or against the inside of one of the stays, even though the friction be inaudible, he will sense that there is something amiss. And that means that he will want to know what it is.

Lubrication

Many, though not all, cycle-makers send their products out from the factories properly lubricated and adjusted. In any case, a reputable cycle-dealer will make sure that every machine he sells is in that condition when he hands it over to the customer who buys it. It is then up to the cyclist himself to see that lubrication and adjustment are continued as and when necessary.

There are several parts of a cycle that obviously have to be lubricated, and normally they are provided with nipples or oil-holes of one type or another. If nipples are fitted, the lubricant, whether oil or grease, must be injected by means of a special gun; in other cases it can be simply introduced a drop at a time from a small oil-can. In any case, the purpose of lubrication should be to ensure that the parts concerned are neither dry nor swimming in lubricant.

The only satisfactory system to follow is to oil frequently but in really small doses, using a good-quality

D

cycle oil, unless the bearings are packed with grease, in which case replacement of the lubricant need not be done anything like so frequently. If too much oil is injected into a bearing, such as those in the wheels or the bottom bracket, the surplus will run down the spokes or the cranks, where it may be a nuisance, and in any case is a waste. Only by following the rule of " a little but often " can the cycle-owner make sure that he is keeping his machine well oiled without being messy.

The obvious places where a cycle should be lubricated are the bearings in the wheels, the pedals and the bottom bracket. Those are the spots normally fitted with oilers. Less obviously in need of lubrication, and quite often not fitted with the means to inject lubricant, are the bearings in the steering-head, yet they, too, should be given regular attention. If they are not packed with grease and are not fitted with oil-holes or nipples, the oil has to be persuaded to enter between the upper and lower cups of each bearing. That is usually less difficult in the case of the upper bearing, though some of the modern types of head-fitting embody locking-rings that cover the bearing, and it may then be necessary to slacken them slightly and turn the cycle upside down in order to get the oil into the desired place.

In any case, it will almost certainly be necessary to " stand the bike on its head " in order to get oil into the lower bearing. It is, in fact, better to pack the bearings with grease, if they are not fitted with oilers. Then they can be left without attention for months—maybe even years if the cycle is not used a great deal.

Other parts of a cycle also require lubrication from time to time, though they are not fitted with any kind of oiler because they are both visible and accessible. They include all the places where one metal rubs against another. An obvious example is the braking system, though of course oil must always be prevented from getting on to the actual braking surfaces.

The pack-horse bridge

MILL DALE.

If the brake transmission is that incorporating a series of rods and levers, as in the case of the stirrup brakes usually fitted to roadster machines, the points at which lubrication is required include the eyelets on the handle-bar, in which the brake-levers turn, as well as the little spindles on which the quadrants are mounted. In the case of cable-operated brakes, the pivots on which the levers turn should be lubricated from time to time, as well as the parts of the actual brake where there is metal-to-metal friction (as between the two arms of side-pull callipers, for instance), and the cable itself should also receive attention.

To oil a brake-cable is admittedly not easy, but it is well worth doing. Not only does it reduce friction con-siderably, but it also protects the wire strands of the cable from invisible rust, which might otherwise lead to unsuspected weakening of a very important fitting. The best way to oil the cable is to remove the brake-lever end of it from the handle-bar and hold it up, so that oil can be induced to run down the inside of the cable covering. It is a slow job, but once it has been thoroughly done it does not have to be repeated so often as the lubrication of some other parts of the cycle.

The control cables of variable gearing devices also require lubrication at appropriate intervals, as do the gear mechanisms themselves. In the case of hub gears, the oil (only very thin oil is suitable) is normally intro-duced through a single oiler in the hub wheel, but some models also incorporate a second oiler at one end of the hub (between the spindle and the spoke-heads).

Derailleur gears call for lubrication at several points, though it is comparatively rare for oilers to be provided. There are the bearings of the chain-tension sprockets, the pivots and pulleys in the control transmission and possibly also a helical spring in the chain-shift mechanism, the coils of which slide over one another and will work more smoothly if there is a thin film of oil between them. Though it is impossible to indicate all the

places that require oiling for all the various kinds of
gearing, it is not difficult to detect them if they are
examined.

Finally, the chain will work much more efficiently,
quietly and smoothly if it is given its fair proportion of
lubricant. Unfortunately, the chain is usually either
neglected altogether until it protests and has to be oiled
to stop the squeaking, or it is lavishly swilled with oil
whenever the owner's eyes light on the oil-can, with the
result that the rear stays, the lower part of the seat-
tube, the chainwheel and cranks are spattered with
dirty oil, and probably some gets on to his clothes.
(It is sometimes said that the simplest way to tell
whether anyone dressed in out-door costume is a
rambler or a cyclist is to look at his socks; the cyclist's
will be oil-stained.)

There is really no need to take the extreme care that
some clubmen do of their cycle chains, washing them
periodically in a bath of paraffin and then immersing
them in warm molten grease so that it will enter the
interior of every link. If the chain is brushed or rubbed
with a cloth, to remove surface dirt, and then intelligently oiled, it will be well enough protected until the
time when dust and dirt have again accumulated on it.
The treatment can then easily be repeated. But
intelligent oiling means distributing the oil thinly and
evenly over all the links—not flooding the chainwheel
and sprockets in the hope that some at least of the
lubricant will get into the right spots.

General Maintenance

If you bought your new bicycle from a reputable
dealer, it will have been delivered to you in good condition. Before handing it over to you he would see that
the bearings were correctly adjusted, that the wheels
were true and that none of the spokes were slack, that
the mudguards were securely attached and had no bent
stays, that the brakes were working smoothly, that the

tyres were really hard, and so on. He would, in fact,
check every component and accessory for you and
satisfy himself that each one was everything that it
should be.

It is now up to you, the owner of this brand-new
perfect bicycle, to keep it in that condition. It will not
remain perfect for long if you do not take care of it.
Very gradually, and without being noticed unless you
make a regular habit of checking adjustments, the bearings will become slack, the chain will become slack, the
saddle-leather will become slack, the mudguard-stays
will work loose, and so will the brakes and the gear-
control. If, however, you keep an eye on all these items
in the first few months of the cycle's life, and make the
necessary adjustments as soon as they become necessary,
the need for further attention will be postponed for a
much longer time. A new bicycle needs more attention
in that respect than one that has been well cared for over
a number of years.

We will assume, therefore, that you are going to give
your new cycle all the attention it deserves. What can
you do besides cleaning and lubricating it whenever
necessary? The best way to answer that question is
to take the main parts of the bicycle in turn and see
what is likely to happen if they are neglected. We
cannot, in a book like this, give a detailed technical
description of every component and accessory on the
market, so the comments and advice must be in general
terms.

You yourself can, however—and certainly should—
get from the makers of the various items that have gone
into the construction of your cycle, the leaflets telling
how they are constructed and how to keep them perfectly adjusted and maintained.

All the manufacturers of good-quality cycle components and accessories publish some kind of literature
to help the users to get the best out of their products.
So do not overlook this opportunity to get excellent

expert advice on the various parts of your machine.   If, for instance, your cycle is fitted with a variable gear, read the maker's instruction-and-maintenance leaflet and follow the advice it gives you.

Similarly, if the hubs of your cycle are not actually made by the manufacturers of the machine and not dealt with in the literature supplied by them, write to the hub-maker for whatever literature he has available.   You may find that he does not want you to adjust your hubs so that there is no play at all, but to leave the merest trace of slackness in them.   It will certainly pay you to know everything that the makers have taken the trouble to put into print.

The Frame

If your cycle was in satisfactory condition when you bought it, nothing short of a severe bump or gross ill-treatment will put the frame out of truth afterwards, and unless the machine is involved in an accident there is no need to worry about it—apart, of course, from taking care of the enamel.

A collision may have more serious effects than are obvious to the casual observer.   Suppose, for instance, you have collided with something substantial and solid. If the front wheel and fork are damaged, it will be obvious, and you will immediately realise the need to have the necessary repairs done by a skilled man.   At the same time, however, the frame itself may have been seriously damaged, but with nothing much to show. So you will carefully examine it to see if the frame is distorted or out of truth in any direction.

You will also run your fingers along the frame tubes, feeling for dents or ripples, especially in the top tube and down tube near their junction with the lugs that link them to the steering-head.   If such an inspection reveals anything out of the ordinary, you should consult a capable repairer.   He will be able to tell you whether the damage is serious or not.

Head Bearings

Sooner of later slackness will develop in the steering-head. If you are really observant you will detect it in the very early stages, because when you apply the front brake you will have the feeling that the frame and the front wheel do not pull up exactly together. Then, sitting on the stationary machine and applying the front brake quite hard, you will rock the cycle to and fro while carefully watching the little space between the upper and lower parts of the ball-races. If there is indeed any slackness, you will then be able to detect the movement.

Later on, when the play in the bearings has become more serious, you will feel it every time you take hold of the centre of the handle-bar and lift it up: the bar will rise a fraction of a second before the rest of the cycle, and there will be a distinct feeling of looseness.

As soon as slackness in the head-bearings has been detected, it should be removed. Whatever type of head-fitting is used, the necessary adjustment is in principle the same: the upper part of the bearing has to be screwed down so that it fits more snugly on the balls held in the lower part. If the fitting is the type embodying a large clip, the nut on the clip must be loosened so that the adjustment may be made by turning the upper ring with the appropriate tool—one with a curved end that has a square tooth in it to fit into a corresponding notch in the ring. Then the clip is returned to its proper position and the nut tightened up again.

Other types of head-fittings make use of various types of adjusting- and locking-rings, but the mechanism is quite obvious when they are examined.

If the bearings are tightened up too much, the handle-bar will be difficult to turn; if it is not tightened enough, there will still be some play. The ideal is an absence of play without too much tightness in the movement of the handle-bar: a slight stiffness may not be a disadvantage.

Bottom Bracket

The spindle that passes through the bottom bracket, and to which the pedal-cranks are attached, is supported by two bearings, one at each end. When slackness develops in those bearings it is felt by the rider as a slight though definite rocking of the cranks, and as soon as that form of play is suspected the bearing should be inspected. By taking hold of the left-hand pedal-crank and gently rocking it sideways (i.e. to and from the cycle frame), you can satisfy yourself whether there is actual slackness in the bearing or not. If there is, you will correct it by slackening the locking-ring on the left-hand end of the bracket (again using the special tool) and then turning the inner ring in the opposite direction as far as is necessary, and finally tightening up the locking-ring once more.

Loose cranks due to slight slackness of the cotter-pin nut are also detected by the sensation they produce on the rider's feet as he pedals. At certain points the foot rocks slightly in a forward direction. The cure is to tighten up the appropriate nut.

Wheels

Probably no part of a cycle deteriorates more quickly or more seriously than the wheels if the machine is not cared for and maintained in good order. The bearings cannot be expected to remain in perfect adjustment for ever without attention, but a distressingly large number of cycle-owners do neglect them to such an extent that the smooth running of the machine is seriously affected. In some cases the ball-races themselves are so much damaged that it is no longer possible to restore the original mechanical perfection by mere adjustment.

The really serious cyclist therefore keeps an eye on his wheel bearings and adjusts them as necessary. Probably, when slackness begins to develop he feels it in the somewhat " flabby " running of the machine, but even if his

attention is not attracted in that way, he will discover the
trouble as soon as he makes a routine examination of the
wheel.

Inspections of that kind are made at quite frequent
intervals by all careful cyclists. Taking hold of each
wheel in turn, while holding the cycle frame steady,
they try to rock them sideways, just as they tested the
bottom bracket. If there is slackness in the wheel
bearings it will allow the wheels to move from side to
side, although the spindles are firmly held in the forks.

A very slight degree of slackness of that kind is not a
bad thing; in fact, some manufacturers recommend
that their hubs should never be so tightened up that
there is no side play. Anything more than the merest
trace of play, however, should be corrected as soon as
it is detected.

First, the nuts holding the wheel-spindle in the cycle
fork (front or rear) are slackened. Then the locking-nut
on the spindle inside the fork is slackened, so that the
" cone " may be adjusted. The cone is actually part
of the ball bearing, but the surface in contact with the
balls is not visible from outside. The side that is visible
looks like a thick washer or metal cylinder with two
parallel " steps " or " flats " on it, designed to take a
special key.

By means of that key the cones can be turned in a
clockwise direction, to tighten the bearing as much as is
necessary before the locking-nut is once more screwed
up tight. Generally speaking, it is wise not to tighten
the cones as much as seems desirable, because the movement of the locking-nut often produces a further tightening, and so may result in a stiff wheel. Here the ideal
is to obtain a wheel that will revolve perfectly freely,
but with the minimum of side play.

After the wheel bearings have been adjusted, the
spindle-nuts must be tightened up again.

Wheel defects are not all due to maladjustment of the
bearings. The rims may become distorted from one

cause or another, and so interfere very seriously with the free running of the cycle, even if they are not so much out of truth as to foul the brake-blocks or the forks.

Defects in the rims caused by ill treatment of the cycle or by accident are usually immediately obvious; they occur suddenly, and the rider cannot help noticing the difference in the running of the machine compared with what he has hitherto been used to. There is no need to tell him that something requires attention.

Much less obvious, because it usually develops gradually, is the distortion of the rim due to incorrect spoke tension, or possibly the breaking of a spoke. It is unfortunately true that nowadays many cycles are sold with wheels that are not perfect, though they may appear so at first. Before they have been subjected to the strains and shocks that actual use produces, the wheels may seem to be perfectly true and may pass workshop tests without revealing the slightest " wobble ", but a few months later their appearance may be quite different, just because the spoke tension, though even throughout, was not correct in the first place.

In such cases usage produces strains which the spokes cannot resist. The rims become slightly distorted, the strain is increased, and the distortion is magnified. In the end the wheel becomes so misshapen that it fouls the brakes or the fork at some part or other and the rider has to do something about it. If, however, he had been the kind of cyclist who is always inspecting, examining and testing his machine, he would have detected the first signs of the coming trouble and put it right before it became serious.

Whenever a wheel has become distorted, so that one part of the rim wobbles nearer to the brake or fork than the rest of it, the fault should be corrected by judicious use of the nipple key. This is a little implement that fits over the metal nipples which project from the wheel rim and into which the spokes are screwed. By turning the key the spoke may be screwed further into the nipple or withdrawn from it. Users of the nipple key should remember that it really screws the nipple on to the spoke, and so it is the anti-clockwise motion (as seen from the point of view of the spoke) that increases the tension on the spoke and pulls the wheel rim over at that point.

To correct a distorted rim, therefore, it is necessary first of all to locate the point at which the rim approaches too closely to the fork. Then the spokes on the opposite side are tightened up very slightly. The wheel is allowed to spin freely, to show the effect of the increased tension. If the effect is not adequate, it may be necessary to slacken adjoining spokes on the other side. In any case, the operation should be carried out carefully and slowly, the effect of each turn of the nipple key being tested by an inspection of the wheel as it is allowed to spin. If spokes are screwed too far into the nipples they may project inside the rim, pierce the rim tape and puncture the tyre.

When the rim cannot be restored to complete truth by simple adjustment on those lines, the wheel should be taken to a competent cycle repairer. Wheel-building is, in fact, a highly skilled job, and though every serious cyclist should be capable of making minor adjustments, and should, indeed, do so as soon as they become necessary, he should never hesitate to recognise the stage at which the trouble gets beyond him.

Pedals

The bearings in which the pedal-spindles run are similar in principle to those in the wheels, and they are similarly adjusted. The cones and locking-nuts are disclosed when the cover at the outer end of each pedal has been removed.

Tyres

There was a time when cyclists were warned against over-inflating their tyres. In those days it was quite a serious risk to leave a bicycle in the sunshine on a hot summer day, and many a tyre has exploded as a result of over-heating in that way. Nowadays the makers of cycle tyres are much more likely to fear that buyers of their products will harm them by under-inflation. They say that their tyres should be blown up hard, and that is what they really mean. It is the only way to get the maximum service out of them.

The only time when it is reasonable to ride a tyre that is not really hard is when the road conditions are slippery and the tyre is rather smooth, but smooth tyres ought not to be used in such circumstances.

Modern tyres are remarkably tough and can stand a good deal of rough usage. They cannot withstand, though, the extremely sharp points of some of the chippings used for road-repairing. The chippings picked up by the tyres will eventually be forced through the rubber and puncture the air-tube unless they are removed. That is why some cyclists carefully " de-grit " their tyres at the end of the day's ride if they have had to travel over sharp chippings. Others fit tiny chains or pieces of thin wire inside the mudguards, so that they just hang down on to the tyres and so catch any pieces of grit (or tacks) that may have been picked up. Those very useful devices are easily made at home but can in any case be bought from cycle-dealers. They are a good investment.

The Saddle

A good deal of your happiness as a cyclist depends on the use of the kind of saddle that is just right for you, and you did in fact make a very careful choice when selecting the one to be fitted to your cycle. With very little trouble indeed you can keep it in perfect condition.

Never leave your machine standing in the rain so that the top of the saddle becomes sodden. If you do, it will almost certainly stretch and sag. The shape will become distorted, and you will not be able to restore it exactly to its original perfection.

Admittedly the slackness in the leather or other material can largely be taken up by turning the adjusting nut under the saddle-nose, but nevertheless the resultant shape will not be completely satisfactory. Some of the transverse tension will have been lost for ever, and what was once a flat surface will have degenerated into a ridge. It therefore pays to see that your saddle is never allowed to get really wet, and it is quite a good idea to treat it with a water-proofing substance, which you can buy from your cycle-dealer.

New saddles sometimes develop a rather irritating squeak or creaking noise after they have been ridden for a few months. Usually this can be cured by lubricating the underside between the crescent-shaped cantle plate and the back.

Brakes

Obviously, whatever form of brakes are fitted to your bicycle, the braking surface will wear away in time and will have to be renewed. Before that is necessary, however, the brakes should be frequently adjusted so that there is no play in the brake-levers, but without making the operation of the brakes too fierce.

If the brakes are not periodically adjusted in that way (the adjustment varies with the make and type of brake), the looseness in the transmission will produce vibration at a number of points, especially where there are pivots of one kind or another. If that is allowed to continue, the time will come when the original tautness in the transmission cannot be restored by mere adjustment and there will be almost constant chattering of the brake-levers—a state of affairs that no conscientious cyclist can tolerate.

Mudguards

Lack of attention to the mudguard fastenings will similarly result in slackness, with consequent vibration and rattle. If it is allowed to continue, the rivets fastening the stays to the mudguard proper may become incurably loose, but there is no excuse for such a condition. It can be prevented if the owner of the cycle will spend a few seconds with a screwdriver now and then.

The Chain

When your new cycle was handed over to you, the chain was nicely adjusted. There was about half an inch of play (up and down movement) on the upper run of the chain midway between chainwheel and rear sprocket. Before long, though, the play becomes greater, because chains do stretch slightly in use, and if it exceeds one inch it should be reduced by moving the wheel a little farther back in the rear fork.

With most machines all that is necessary is to undo the nuts at each end of the rear wheel-spindle, pull the wheel back until the chain tension is satisfactory, and then tighten the nuts again, taking care that the wheel is kept perfectly central in the fork. Some cycles are fitted with chain adjusters, so that when the spindle nuts have been loosened the wheel can be pulled backwards mechanically by turning the little nuts on the adjusters. Such fittings are rather uncommon nowadays, though.

When a cycle is equipped with some form of derailleur gearing system it is not necessary to adjust the chain tension after it has once been settled by the adoption of a chain of appropriate length. The gearing system incorporates an automatic chain-tensioning device as part of the mechanism for transferring the chain from one sprocket to another.

CHAPTER XIII

GETTING ABOUT ON A BICYCLE

THE idea that cycling is hard work has been killed. You now know that it is hard work only when it is done by an unskilled rider or on an inefficient machine.

To anyone who has taught himself cycling and possesses a well-made and well-kept bicycle, it is the pleasantest form of physical exercise, much less tiring than walking. As a recreation it is in a class by itself, combining physical and intellectual pleasures in whatever proportions the cyclist himself may prefer. At one end of the scale, cycling is a real he-man's sport; at the other it is the ideal recreation for the elderly philosopher who loves to potter around the country lanes.

Cycling means different things to different people and even to the same people at different times. To young and lusty riders it represents the pure delight of physical exertion (and possibly also the boisterous companionship of other young people with the same delight in hard riding). Enthusiasts of that kind have a natural interest in cycle racing, and when they go touring they may like to bash along the main roads or go mudlarking or pass-storming.

Older cyclists usually have quieter ideas of touring. They are not in the least attracted by main roads. For them the physical pleasure of cycling is not predominant and, so far as it exists, comes more from the ability to cover long distances and to climb hills easily. They know that physical pleasure is not the only joy to be derived from cycling. They delight in travel and exploration, and find them more and more delightful as the years go by.

Now that you, too, have learned a great deal about cycling, you will appreciate the value of the bicycle as a means of getting about.   At first, no doubt, you will be content just to explore the countryside in the neighbourhood of your own home, and you will find there far greater interests than you ever imagined.

It does not matter where you live : even if your home is in the centre of London, you are within cycling distance of open country where there are lovely villages, quiet lanes, historic old buildings with wonderful stories for those who will take the trouble to discover them, as well as fields, woods, hedgerows and water-courses offering unlimited pleasures to the cyclist who will use his eyes and his ears.   The cyclist is better equipped than any other traveller for studying the natural beauties and charm of country life because he travels silently and yet is not so limited in range as is the walker.

Once you have begun to take an interest in the countryside on your own doorstep you will never be satisfied.   There will always be something new to discover over the hill or round the corner.   You will go on wanting to know what there is to be seen and to be learned and to be enjoyed farther afield.   You will, in fact, become a tourist, and will realise that, even if you live to be a hundred, you will never be able to exhaust the delights that cycle touring—getting about on a bicycle— has to offer you.

Let us suppose you have just begun to realise what a wonderful instrument of travel the bicycle is, and that you have decided to use it, for the first time, for a long journey out into the country.   You have perhaps heard that members of cycling clubs regularly ride a hundred miles every Sunday, and have convinced yourself that if they can do it you can too.

Today you are going to put your convictions into practice.   Early in the morning, after a good breakfast, you set off.   In the bag behind your saddle you have packed sandwiches and a thermos flask, so that you can enjoy an alfresco lunch.   When it comes to tea-time you will buy a meal in some convenient café.

Your bicycle is in excellent mechanical condition, your cape is strapped on top of the saddle-bag, your repair outfit and tools are in the side pocket of the saddle-bag and you yourself are feeling fit and ready for anything. Away you go.

In the first hour you cover fifteen miles, for you know all about pedalling efficiency and have adopted a good riding position. There is no reason why you shouldn't keep up the same pace all through the day. Or so you think.

Two hours later you are not so sure. Your average has fallen to less than thirteen miles an hour and you are beginning to feel tired. It seems very doubtful whether you will be able to do a hundred miles, after all.

Many an enthusiastic but inexperienced cyclist has set off with similar confidence and discovered that he still had something to learn before he could ride easily and confidently all day. Tired and dejected at the end of a smaller mileage than he expected to accomplish, he has asked himself why, if the others can do it so cheerfully and so easily, he cannot too.

The answer cannot be given in a few words. It comprises several truths, some of which are only revealed by experience. In the first place, the really experienced cyclist knows that if he is to make a long journey he must resist the temptation to force the pace in the early stages. It is so easy to believe, when first setting out, that you are in unusually good form, but even if that happens to be true it is more prudent to save as much energy as possible for the later stages of the ride.

Anybody can force himself to ride a steep hill at the beginning of the day, but the wise rider will probably decide to walk even a moderate hill within the first twenty miles. Similarly he will resist the temptation to ride fast, and will never " ride on an empty stomach ".

" Hunger Knock "

Tiredness when cycling is less common than is generally supposed.   Quite often what is assumed to be fatigue is actually a manifestation of hunger.

That is a truth which the experienced cyclist never forgets, but which the novice often has to learn through suffering and distress.   In cycling-club circles the exaggerated weariness and muscular failure caused by " riding on an empty stomach " are known by various names, such as " the bonk ", " the knock ", " a parcel ", " the sags ", and other semi-humorous names for a condition that in itself is far from funny.

When that condition arises it is often difficult to persuade the victim that he or she is really suffering from hunger, and not from real fatigue.   Nevertheless, if the trouble is not so far advanced as to cause nausea and make eating unpleasant, something to eat will usually produce a wonderful recovery, especially if the " something to eat " contains sugar in an easily assimilable form.

In this matter, as in many others, prevention is far better than a cure, and so the wise cyclist will always eat at the first signs of hunger.   Big meals are not to be recommended, but adequate food when appropriate— that means sooner rather than later—is essential.

Another lesson that has to be learnt before the cyclist can accomplish long rides is the importance of not wearing himself out by needless exertion in hill-climbing or fighting a head-wind.   It is usually better to climb a hill by using the lowest gear that can be turned without discomfort.   Inexperienced riders work on the opposite principle: they change to a lower gear only when they cannot continue to pedal on the one in use.

That again is a principle which the novice may be reluctant to accept until experience has shown him how sound it is.   In hilly country especially, young and enthusiastic riders are apt to under-estimate the value of using low gears. Of course it does not matter so long as, at the end of the day, they are quite happy with what they have done, but older riders—and especially those who have taken up cycling comparatively late in life—will find that the intelligent use of low gears enables them to accomplish, without undue fatigue, long rides which would otherwise be beyond their capacity.

"Taking it easy" is perhaps even more important when facing a head-wind. The greater the speed of the rider, the more obstructive and tiring is the wind.

The effect of wind resistance is directly proportional to the square of the rider's speed—and that means his "air speed". He cannot control the actual force of the wind, but he can moderate his own speed, and so reduce the wind's effect on him. His ride will take longer, but he will at any rate complete it without distress, whereas if he tried to maintain his normal average riding speed the extra energy entailed might prove distressingly tiring.

The importance of "taking it easy" is appreciated by experienced tourists not only in its application to the physical side of cycling, but also in its bearing on their whole outlook. They know, for instance, that they can in effect frighten themselves into a state of tiredness by constantly thinking of the distance still to be covered. They therefore take each mile of the journey as it comes, and do not dwell on those ahead.

At the foot of a hill the wise rider does not think of the long climb before him, but just keeps on "turning them round" on a conveniently low gear, and in due course reaches the top. If he were to keep looking up towards the summit, comparing the distance to be covered with that already accomplished, and wondering whether he would be able to make it, he probably would not.

In teaching yourself cycling you have to train not only your body but also your mind, and in mental training, as in muscular exercise, practice makes perfect.

Going Further Afield

When you have discovered for yourself how much pleasure there is in " getting about on a bicycle " and how easy it is when you know how, it will not be long before you start thinking of making longer journeys.

You may still limit your riding to Saturday and Sunday excursions, but increase the scope of each day's ride by taking the train to some convenient new starting point. In that way you may be able to open up a good deal of new territory, but of course the success of the idea depends on the convenience with which you can get a train from your home station to a suitable point for starting cycling. If you are lucky, there may be a train at a suitable time in the direction you wish to take, but that sort of good fortune is not too common, and in any case may not endure when you decide to strike out in a fresh direction.

Train assistance is undoubtedly helpful in some circumstances, but its usefulness is limited, and is always coupled with the trouble of putting a bicycle on to the train and disembarking it a little later on—to say nothing of the cost of the tickets for bicycle and passenger.

A more convenient method of extending your riding scope is to set off on the Saturday, spend the night at a youth hostel or a C.T.C. house, and ride home by an indirect route on the Sunday. That may well be cheaper than taking the train, but in any case it will certainly be more pleasant.

Week-end excursions call for more planning than a one-day trip, and such questions as clothing and what to take by way of luggage now begin to be important. You have, in fact, reached the stage when you ought to examine the basic principles of successful cycle touring, which, after all, is merely a logical extension of the cycling week-end.

CHAPTER XIV

CYCLE TOURING

ONE of the greatest events in the cyclist's life—comparable with that delightful occasion when he took delivery of his first " real " bicycle—is the day when he sets off for the first time on a cycle tour.

Even if he is only going away for a long week-end, when he leaves home and pushes off towards the hitherto unexplored country that he has chosen for this great adventure, he cannot help feeling excited by the enterprise.

Yet setting off on a cycle tour is so simple. The rider does not have to worry about railway time-tables or the crowds of harassed passengers who throng the stations at holiday time. He does not have to wonder whether he will " get a seat ". He does not have to wait until he " gets there " before he can relax and begin to really enjoy himself. His enjoyment starts on his own doorstep. Some cycle tourists say it begins at the moment when they first think of plans for their tours.

Planning is important and, when properly carried out, ensures that the tourist will get the greatest possible enjoyment from his holiday.

Obviously one of the questions that have to be settled during the preliminary planning stage is where to go. Others are what to take and how to take it.

The question of where to go depends on what length of holiday the tourist has available, what kind of country appeals to him, and how far he likes to ride in a day. Young riders, naturally enough, are more interested in going places than in seeing things. They are also generally capable of riding long distances in difficult country and at good average speeds. Older people, on the other hand, prefer as a rule to give themselves plenty of time for looking around.

Planning the Tour

Let us suppose that you are planning your first cycle tour of any length. You may have decided to go to the Lake District, to North Wales, or the Scottish Highlands, or the Yorkshire Dales or down into Devon and Cornwall. In any case, whatever your age and whatever your physique may be, you must base your plans on the assumption that, if you are at all interested in the scenery through which you are passing, the average daily distance you will cover will be less than you are used to accomplishing on an ordinary day's ride in familiar country near home. And if your home country is less hilly than your proposed touring-ground, you must allow for a further reduction in speed and mileage.

When you have decided how far you can expect to ride each day, and how many days you will have available for riding, you can draw up your preliminary itinerary.

The simplest method is to take a motoring map of the area and work out a route based on the main roads shown on it. That is easier, but very much less satisfactory, than if you take a larger-scale map, such as the half-inch Bartholomew, and draft out an itinerary that deliberately avoids the main roads.

A by-lanes route will take more time in the planning stage, and when you come to do the actual riding you may have to stop now and again to check your position with the map, but whether you believe it or not at the beginning of your touring career, you will learn from experience that it is far better to travel quietly along secondary roads, in unspoiled country, than to join the hurrying hordes of vehicles that crowd the great highways.

In the lanes you can talk to your companion or think quietly to yourself, but on the main arterial roads the rush and roar of the faster traffic isolate you from con-

versational contact with other people—unless you are
prepared to shout at one another—and make it well-
nigh impossible for you to think of anything but the
desirability of getting to your destination as quickly as
possible.

" Getting there " is the purpose for which these great
highways were designed and constructed, and on the rare
occasions when you, too, are concerned only with reaching
some particular place as quickly as possible you may think
it worth while to put up with the dust and the din and
ride as fast as you can along main roads.   You may even
think it worth doing that in order to reach the heart of
your touring-ground with the minimum delay.   If so,
well and good: the discomfort may be justifiable as the
price of time saved.   But once you reach the area where
you are going to spend your holiday, then use your map
and your intelligence to enable you to keep as far as
possible from the busier roads.

Clothing

Now comes the question of what luggage to take.   To a
large extent it depends on what clothing you are going to
wear while cycling and what you need when off the
bicycle.   Some tourists, of the more spartan kind, are
quite content to wear in the evening, when their riding is
done, the same clothes as those in which they did the
day's cycling.   Others prefer to make a complete
change, discarding the shorts and open-necked shirt they
wore when on the bicycle and replacing them with long
trousers and a shirt and collar and tie of a rather more
formal kind.

It is mainly a question of temperament and circumstances.   The young hard-rider who stays at youth
hostels is not likely to attach the same importance as an
older rider using hotels to the ability to don ordinary
clothes every evening.   He may, in fact, find it difficult
to understand why he should encumber himself with the
weight of so much spare clothing when he knows he will

spend his evenings in the company of other young people dressed like himself in open-air costume.

Each tourist must decide for himself how much change of clothing he must allow for when packing his holiday luggage. If he wants to take virtually a spare suit of clothes, it is entirely his own affair, and he is just as much entitled to do as he likes in that respect as he is to choose his own touring-districts and regulate his daily mileages to suit his wishes. There is, however, one aspect of this clothing question which has to be considered in advance by every cycle tourist, whether he believes in taking a change of clothing or not. He must provide for occasions when he will need extra warmth.

In this country especially the weather can be most unreliable, and the tourist who has left home under a blue sky and ridden for several days in summer sunshine may nevertheless come face to face with quite different circumstances and need to protect himself against cold northerly or easterly winds. Complete changes in the weather have always to be taken into account when planning a tour, especially in spring and autumn. The wise tourist therefore makes certain before leaving home that he is equipped to meet not only continuous and heavy rain, but also really cold weather.

Protection against rain is a simple matter. Modern waterproof clothing designed for use by cyclists is good, reasonably light, not at all bulky and, by modern standards, moderately priced. It is possible for a cyclist to equip himself with a large cape, a pair of leggings, and sou'wester or other head covering, and so ensure protection against long and heavy downpours. When not in use, such equipment can be carried in the straps on top of the saddle-bag or in some other equally convenient and accessible position.

The simplest precaution against cold weather is a spare jersey or pullover. It need not be a bulky garment, but it will give a good deal of protection against the cold. If the weather is so unexpectedly cold that the

donning of a spare pullover is not enough, then the
rider may find it necessary to put on other extra clothing.
It is better to wear two shirts at once, and even to make
use of a cape when it is not raining, rather than shiver
miserably because the weather has turned much colder
than had been expected.

Essential Luggage

Clothes are not the only items of luggage that the
tourist has to carry, although for an extended holiday
they will probably take up most of the room. Other
things for which provision must be made include not only
the usual tool-kit and repair outfit, but also such spares
as bulbs for the lamps and a chain-fastening link. It is
quite likely that they will not be needed, but it is
obviously possible that the need for them may arise
when you are in some remote corner many miles from the
nearest cycle repair shop. It is also a good idea to carry
a coil of thin wire, some insulating tape, a small screwdriver and a pair of pliers.

Other things you will need include the appropriate
maps and perhaps a guide-book, if you are interested in
looking up architectural and historical data on the spot,
and maybe a camera or sketching material.

Whatever quantity of luggage you take with you on
tour, it will comprise a certain number of articles that
must be readily accessible. Obviously you will want to
be able to get at your cape and leggings without having
to unpack all your spare shirts. Similarly, if you have a
spot of mechanical trouble, you will find it much more
convenient if you can immediately produce tools and
repair outfit from a separate place to which they can be restored after use without disturbing the rest of the luggage.

Your luggage will also include other things which
should be kept fairly handy, even though they are not
likely to be needed in a desperate hurry. Such articles
as your first-aid kit (perhaps nothing more than a tin
containing a few bandages) and soap and towel may be

wanted during the course of a day's riding, and so should be reasonably near at hand. Similarly, the spare pullover, carried as a precaution against a sudden change in the weather, ought not to be buried beneath all your spare underclothing.

A tourist's luggage can be divided into three kinds of articles—those that are likely to be needed en route; those that will be required at the end of the day's riding; and spare clothing which will be brought into use from time to time during the holiday. That classification should be kept in mind when packing the luggage, so that each article may be obtained when required without needlessly disturbing other things. If the three kinds of luggage can be carried in separate bags, so much the better.

When the whole of the luggage has to be accommodated in an ordinary saddle-bag plus a smaller bag fitted to the front of the handle-bar, it is best to use the front bag for the articles you are likely to need en route. Then you can, if you wish, take off the saddle-bag alone when putting your bicycle away for the night and going to your bedroom. In that case your spare clothes will be placed, carefully folded, at the bottom of the saddle-bag, with pyjamas or nightdress on top of them, and on top of that the garments into which you will change at the end of the day's riding.

By planning your packing in some such systematic manner you will cut down the time that has to be spent sorting things out at the end of a ride and putting them back into their proper places next morning. You will also reduce to a minimum the risk of spare clothing becoming grubby or creased before being worn.

Foreign Touring

Interest in foreign travel has increased very considerably in recent years, and every summer thousands of cyclists leave Britain to spend their holidays touring on the Continent. It is much easier for them to do so

nowadays than it was in the years between the two world
wars. Since 1946 the Cycle Touring Commission of
the Alliance Internationale de Tourisme, which has its
headquarters in London at the offices of the C.T.C.,
has succeeded in removing the obstacles to free movement which previously confronted the cycle tourist.
Now he can freely enter almost every European country
without being called upon to pay duty on his bicycle or
to provide himself in advance with a document of ex-
emption. Although two countries (Austria and Switzerland) still keep a check on the entry and exit of tourists'
bicycles, it is the Customs officers themselves who provide
the tourist with the necessary clearance document
(entirely without cost) to enable him to bring his machine
out of the country at the end of his holiday.

It is possible for anybody to cross the Channel and
start cycling on the Continent so long as he or she has a
passport and an appropriate amount of foreign money.
It is, however, much better for the intending tourist to
become a member of the C.T.C. and seek the assistance
of its Foreign Travel Department before leaving Britain.
The C.T.C., because of its affiliation to the A.I.T., can
supply members with up-to-date and accurate information about conditions in other countries, and can also
give them a ticket of introduction to foreign touring
clubs, whose assistance they can invoke without cost
while resident on their territory.

The C.T.C. will, in fact, not only give you expert
advice on the planning of your tour, but will also obtain
for you, if you wish, your passport and your foreign
currency, as well as your boat and rail tickets, and supply
you with appropriate maps and guide-books.

Another facility provided by the C.T.C. for its members is the opportunity to get into touch with suitable
touring companions by means of a free announcement in
the Club's monthly magazine, or to join one of the
organised parties that are led on holiday tours by
experienced leaders.

CHAPTER XV

CYCLE CAMPING

At the end of each day the cycle tourist must find somewhere to spend the night. He has a greater chance of success if he is alone than if he is accompanied by companions, but even the lone wolf may find it difficult to obtain shelter for the night during the holiday season in some of the more popular touring districts.

That is why some tourists habitually plan their routes very carefully and take the precaution of booking accommodation in advance for the end of each day's " stage ". Others prefer to book for a week or a fortnight at one particular place and spend their holiday cycling out into the surrounding country and returning each evening to their chosen roost. This procedure is called centre touring in Britain; across the Channel they speak of it as star touring.

The need to find accommodation for the night does limit the freedom of the tourist who likes to go where and as far as he pleases each day, and in some circumstances it may even develop into a serious problem.

There is, however, one type of cyclist for whom such problems do not exist—the cycle camper. Generally speaking, he can spend the night wherever he may choose. As evening approaches, he does not have to make his way towards some centre of human habitation, hoping he may find there an inn with an unoccupied room. In fact, he avoids anything resembling a " built-up area ", and looks for some quiet spot where he may pitch his tent and spend the night in peace, to waken next morning in the delightful freshness of the open air.

Unfortunately, the advantages of cycle camping are less obvious than are the apparent disadvantages.

Every cyclist realises, as soon as the subject of camping

is broached, that it must mean carrying around some
extra weight. Some of them immediately think as
well of the inevitable loss of " home comforts " and,
without making a practical test, a number of them are
inclined to say that whatever the possible advantages
may be, they are heavily outweighed by the inevitable
disadvantages. On the other hand, those who have
tried camping, especially when touring in remote places,
are usually reluctant to go back to the limited freedom
and enjoyment of the more conventional kinds of
habitation.

Freedom and Mobility

The cyclist who takes up camping generally does so
because he is attracted by the obvious advantage of
being able to spend the night wherever he may happen
to be, and especially away from towns. His tent is an
aid to cycle touring, and for him camping is not in itself
the major attraction. Whereas ardent campers, for
whom camping as such is the chief pleasure, thoroughly
enjoy being dwellers in tents whenever they get the
opportunity, and derive a great deal of pleasure from
preparing and cooking their own meals, the cycle
camper attaches much more importance to being able to
get up in the morning and continue his journey at a
reasonably early hour.

No doubt some cycle campers, though essentially
tourists at heart, do take a delight in being able to
prepare excellent meals for themselves, but most of them
are satisfied so long as they have at hand the means of
making a good cup of tea or warming up a tin of baked
beans. They can always enjoy picnic meals en route or,
if they feel like it, buy a properly cooked meal in a
restaurant. They do not have to carry around with them
bulky kitchen utensils, which for them would be a serious
encumbrance, although they are the necessary equipment of the camper who " stays put " in one place for
some considerable time.

All that the touring cycle camper needs is a tent, something to sleep on and in, a simple form of spirit or paraffin stove, a water container and wash-basin and the bare minimum of cutlery and light metal " crockery ".

It will pay him to buy some of the really first-class light-weight equipment that is offered nowadays by the leading makers of tents and camping accessories. Their products are not only light but also really good. Though it may be possible to obtain tents of similar shape and size at less cost by buying from hardware dealers or garden-supply stores, there is no doubt whatsoever that the dearer articles are far better value for money. They are not only much lighter—an important point to the cycle camper—but are made of material that is more durable and considerably more waterproof.

Tents

There are two types of tent suitable for cyclists. Perhaps the most popular is that using only a single supporting pole. Next in popularity is the simple ridge pattern, using a vertical pole at each end. A fly-sheet, which is a kind of second roof to cover the tent itself, and so give extra protection against the weather, is by no means a luxury.

A tent fitted with a fly-sheet is partially insulated against changes of temperature in the outside air— shaded against extreme heat, and to some extent protected against the cold. In wet weather the occupant of such a tent can move about in it with far greater freedom than if the tent were not protected with a fly-sheet. It does not matter if his head comes into contact with the roof of the tent, whereas if there were no fly-sheet, every time he touched the inside of the tent he would start a trickle of rain percolating through.

Although a fly-sheet is not absolutely indispensable, a ground-sheet is. It may be nothing more than a sheet of oil-silk or vulcanised canvas big enough to fit under the sleeping-bag, but preferably it should cover the whole floor-space of the tent. In some of the more modern light-weight tents it is permanently attached to the tent walls. Tents with " built-in " ground-sheets of that kind are naturally free from draughts, and the work of pitching and striking the tent is simplified.

It is possible to buy a tent, giving 5 ft. of head room and covering an area of 7 ft. by 5 ft., together with ground-sheet and fly-sheet and the necessary poles and pegs (made of aluminium alloy) weighing altogether less than 7 lb. A good-quality light-weight sleeping-bag need not weigh more than $2\frac{1}{2}$ lb.

Aluminium alloys are used a good deal in the making of light-weight camping equipment nowadays, and so the total weight to be carried around by the cycle camper can be kept within reasonable proportions. Nevertheless, the rider must not forget that he is, in fact, carrying a greater load than ordinarily, and so, before setting off for a long cycle-camping tour, he should make sure that his bicycle is not too highly geared, especially if he intends to visit mountainous country.

Carrying the Kit

Experience will teach the cycle-camping novice many things which may not seem obvious at first sight. Not only will he learn the importance of having suitably low gears available for use in difficult circumstances, but he will also learn how best to pack his luggage and camp kit on his bicycle. Even though modern camping equipment is not unduly heavy, it can be rather bulky, and therefore, unless it is skilfully packed, something of a handicap. Intelligent distribution of the total load between the two wheels of the bicycle is important. It is also desirable to attach the load as near the ground as possible.

Perhaps the best arrangement is to use luggage-carriers on both the front and rear wheels, to which pannier bags may be attached. Naturally the rear wheel will take the greater part of the burden, because of the risk of interference with the steering if bulky loads are attached at the front. In any case, both carriers should be strong and firmly attached to the bicycle. Some of the light-weight carriers made of aluminium alloy and sold for attachment to bicycles by means of clips are quite unsuitable for use by cycle campers. When charged with fully loaded panniers they have a marked tendency to sway from side to side and may, in fact, cause serious accidents. Tubular steel carriers are best, especially if they are brazed on to the cycle frame in such a way that most of the load is carried by the wheel-spindles.

Many cycle campers agree that it is preferable to separate the specific cycling equipment (cape, maps, tools, repair outfit and so on) from the actual camp kit. In that case the cycling gear can be carried either in an ordinary saddle-bag on the front of the handle-bar or in small panniers attached to the front carrier. Then the tent, sleeping-bag and other camping equipment can be accommodated in bigger panniers over the rear wheel. If the panniers are not big enough to take all the luggage, the tent and ground-sheet can be attached on top of the rear carrier.

Any cyclist who is trying camping for the first time would be well advised to make his first venture in the company of a more experienced camper, from whom he can get good advice. Before setting off for his first camp he should also do a little experimenting, to find out the best arrangement for packing his kit. Later on he may make further modifications in the order of packing, but eventually he will discover the most convenient arrangement, which he should then adhere to. Systematic packing will not only save time when pitching tent or striking camp, but if everything has its place it will avoid the annoyance of discovering when the panniers have all been filled and strapped to the machine that something has been overlooked.

E

What has already been said about the importance
of having a good bicycle, maintained in good condition,
for cycle touring is even more important when the
machine is to be used for a camping tour. The tyres
should not only be in excellent condition, but should also
be well chosen to stand rough usage, as the camper is
most likely to develop a fondness for places off the
beaten track.

Where to Camp

The best camp sites are undoubtedly those that are
well away from the towns and other centres of population. Even though the cycle camper may, in his early
days, feel that it is safer to make for recognised camping-
grounds, such as those maintained by the camping and
touring organisations in all the European countries, so
that he may be sure of finding there a suitable water
supply and probably also facilities for buying food,
he will later prefer the really quiet and remote places
where he may pitch his tent in perfect peace and solitude.
By then he will have learned how to select a good camp
site. He will have found, by experience, how important
it is to choose a reasonably level portion of ground, free
from stones. He will also have learnt the wisdom of
making sure, before starting to pitch his tent, that the
selected site is not likely to be haunted by insects—
midges, ants, wasps and so on. It is indeed well worth
while having a good look round for signs of such pests
before it is too late. The noise of heavy traffic on a
nearby main road can also destroy the charm of an
otherwise pleasant camp. Cows in the same field as a
camper are almost certain to upset him, either literally
or metaphorically, before morning.

It is often tempting to pitch a tent by the side of a
stream of clear water, but if, during the night, heavy
rain causes the stream to swell suddenly and invade the
tent, the situation immediately becomes a good deal less
charming. Similarly, a tent pitched in a secluded

The Cross at EYAM.

hollow between grassy slopes may be ideally protected
against the wind, but disastrously situated in the event
of a heavy downpour of rain. For that reason high
ground is usually preferable, but it should be chosen
carefully, so as to avoid a site that is needlessly exposed to
the wind. A camp site surrounded by trees may be
pleasant and shielded, but it is unwise to camp actually
under trees, as anyone will agree who has been so
situated during a rain-storm—the " gentle pitter patter on
the roof " can become unbearable.

With all these points firmly fixed in his mind—
accumulated experience that has become almost in-
stinctive—the camper will look around at the close of the
day for some quiet little corner where he may be per-
mitted to pitch his tent. Permission is most important.

Camper's Code

Good campers always seek permission from the owner
or tenant of the land on which they wish to camp before
actually taking up occupation. They also see that when
they leave the camp site they have not given the slightest
cause for complaint to the owner. They leave no
unsightly indication of their stay, and do not forget to
express their thanks for the facilities that have been
granted to them.

Punctiliousness in that respect is not mere fussiness:
it is the good manners of camping, and the means
whereby the good campers can enhance the name of
camping. Unfortunately, not all campers are good, and
many farmers in this country and abroad have had cause
to regret having given permission for tents to be pitched
on their land. Only campers themselves can help to
overcome the prejudice that has arisen (quite under-
standably) in some quarters. They can do it by seeing
that their own conduct is impeccable and also by in-
ducing others to follow the best examples.

Camping is still largely free from restriction in this
country, but in some foreign countries it is subject to

control. If, therefore, you are thinking of going for a cycle camping tour across the Channel, it will pay you to get in touch with the Camping Club of Great Britain and Ireland or with the Cyclists' Touring Club. Both organisations, through their international affiliations, can provide you with internationally recognised documents, third-party insurance (necessary in some countries), lists of camp sites to which their members are admitted, as well as up-to-date touring information.

CHAPTER XVI

CLUB CYCLING

There are one or two countries where the bicycle is used to a greater extent than it is in Britain. We have, according to reliable estimates, something like ten million bicycles in use by a population of fifty million people, or an average of one bicycle for every five inhabitants. In Holland the corresponding figure is one bicycle between four people, while in Denmark and Sweden it is one between two. But there is no other country where the bicycle is used so much as it is here for pleasure purposes, and there is certainly no other country where cycling-club activities are so well developed.

Everybody who has travelled on British roads at week-ends knows that cycling clubs are a prominent feature of our national life. In summer, especially, many thousands of groups of riders are to be seen travelling merrily along the country lanes, the by-roads or (less commendably) the great highways. Most of the riders are young, and most of the clubs are mixed— jolly parties of happy youths and girls riding gaily coloured bicycles with apparent ease and sometimes with surprising speed.

The fun and the companionship of cycling-club life have an obvious appeal for young people, but perhaps the most ardent club members are those who have grown up in the game. When they were first attracted they were comparatively young, and no doubt looked upon cycling clubs as essentially for young people, but eventually they discovered that cycling-club life is different from many other youthful activities. It is not something that you " grow out of ". In fact, the older you become the more you appreciate the week-ends spent in the company of like-minded friends.

If you yourself have been thinking of joining the local wheelers or the nearest section of the C.T.C., you certainly ought to do so. The mere fact that you have been thinking about it, that the idea has appealed to you, shows that you are the kind of person who will enjoy cycling-club life. We are assuming, of course, that the club you choose is not one specialising in some form of cycling activity in which you are at present not interested. It would obviously be silly for a rider whose chief interest is in pottering around country lanes to enrol as a member of a road club interested mainly in racing and hard riding. You can, however, be sure that, wherever you may live, you are not too far away from a cycling club that will give you just the facilities you want.

Most cycling clubs that provide riding and social facilities have frequent " invitation rides ", and may advertise them in the local newspapers. In any case, such clubs are always glad to welcome a prospective new member who wishes to spend a day with them just to see if he would really fit in. Perhaps he is at heart rather doubtful of his ability to keep up with them on their rides, or not quite sure that their idea of a pleasant day out will coincide with his own.

Let us suppose that you yourself have been thinking about joining a cycling club. You have, in fact, finally decided to go out with them for a trial outing, and are now on your way to their regular meeting-place. You may be a bit shy, for after all it is something of an ordeal to present yourself entirely alone to a group of people who are all well known to one another but know nothing at all about you. You may feel very much like the new boy at school, but (unless there is something seriously wrong with the club you have chosen) you will lose your shyness long before lunch-time. And at the end of the day, when you leave your new pals and they say " Cheerio; see you next week-end ", you will feel (unless there is something seriously wrong with you) that a week is a long time to wait for a reunion with such friendly folk.

Members of cycling clubs are indeed friendly folk. In fact, cyclists in general are friendly, because cycling is a sport, a game, a pastime—call it what you will—that attracts the friendly and co-operative type of person. No one can imagine a cross-grained or sulky individual taking up cycling for pleasure. Nor can anyone who knows anything of cycling clubs imagine one thriving if it is not predominantly a happy family.

Friendliness—companionship—is the chief characteristic of cycling clubs, but it is not by any means the only attraction that they have for their members. Although cycling-club members do not as a rule enrol merely for what they can get out of them, they do, in fact, get a great deal out of them.

The riders who get most out of cycling-club life are those who live in the big cities. In the first place they probably join a cycling club purely for companionship and the physical pleasure of riding a bicycle. Very soon, however, they discover that there is much more in it than that.

Their rides take them out into the open country—easily, quietly and inexpensively—and there they discover that the open country is a very much more interesting place than they had previously imagined. They often find too that their more experienced club mates have become country men at heart and are, in a quiet sort of way, experts on many aspects of country life, able to pass on their knowledge in the friendly, infectious manner that arouses the newcomer's interest. Subjects that previously sounded deadly dull, just because the novice knew nothing of them but their names, may become really exciting when presented by a club-man who is in love with the countryside, its scenery, its hills and villages, and the people who live in it.

A New Outlook

On your trial outing with your chosen club you may find that when they pull up in a village somewhere for elevenses or lunch or tea, or possibly just to have a look round, somebody or other will ask you if you have ever had a look at the Saxon remains in the church crypt, or seen the lovely Norman doorway, or visited the nearby scene of some historic event. And if, up to then, you have not been particularly interested in history or architecture, it is probable that you will discover for the first time that they are not dry-as-dust topics.

The people in the history books were real, no matter how unreally they were presented to you at school, and when somebody reminds you, on the spot, of what they did, their lives and activities begin to sound interesting. It is just the same with buildings: when someone has shown you how to look at them, how to recognise the different historical periods in architectural style, and your imagination has been stirred enough to make you want to know more about the kind of people who were the builders and what sort of lives they led, the word "architecture" ceases to be forbiddingly technical, and the subject changes into something you want to know just a little bit more about.

On purely technical matters the cyclist who is a member of a club has a great advantage over the lone rider. His knowledge is not limited to his own experiences, but he shares the benefit of his fellow-members' experiments.

Any new idea or new gadget that is tried out by a member of a cycling club is naturally of interest to most of the members, and in due course they all know to what extent it has been a success and whether it is worth adopting generally. In that way the individual rider acquires a knowledge that would be entirely beyond his means if he had to obtain it by personal experiment. No ordinary cyclist could afford to try out for instance, one after the other, the different types of cycle brake or even the different kinds of brake-lever, but after some months as a member of a cycling club he will have a very sound knowledge of their respective merits and short-comings.

If the club you decide to join is the C.T.C., which, incidentally, is the biggest in the world, you will not only enjoy all these advantages locally but will also receive a monthly magazine in which cycling questions are discussed with the same freedom and authority as general questions are debated in the correspondence columns of *The Times*. The " Readers in Council " feature of *The C.T.C. Gazette* is very popular—as, of course, are the other contents of this famous cycling journal.

Group Riding

When you go out with a cycling club you will learn why people who from time to time criticise cyclists as a class are usually very ready to exclude club cyclists from their strictures. A club cyclist is generally a good cyclist. Even if he is a little inexperienced and lacking in roadmanship when he first enrols, he will very soon accept and adopt the high standard set by the reputable clubs. Clubs are usually very proud of their reputations, and do everything they can to enhance the good name of cyclists as a whole. In fact, the most severe critics of cycling " yobs " are the cycling clubs.

The C.T.C. gives every new member a copy of a printed code of conduct (reproduced on page 157), but that code does not cover all the rules which have to be observed by members of a club when out riding together.

Riders who go out in groups can only do so safely and without inconvenience to other traffic if they operate as a unit. That is why cycling clubs always have a runs leader or captain, whose job it is to see that the group of which he is in charge rides as a team, and not like a rabble.

Club groups are made up of pairs of riders, and each pair keeps a reasonable distance behind the one in front. Every member of the group has to remember the safety and convenience of the other riders; he must not make sudden changes of direction or speed without warning those behind him, and if he is riding on the outside he must not squeeze his left-hand companion into the side of the road or so hedge him in that he has no room to dodge a pot-hole or any other obstacle.

Obstacles which might not be seen until the last moment by anyone other than the front-rank riders are usually signalled by the captain. In fact, he warns the group as a whole of any reason for changing speed or direction. When he wishes to bring the party to a halt he gives a warning shout and allows some seconds to elapse before actually stopping. In the old days, when cycling-club members all wore uniforms, whistles or bugles were used for this purpose, but nowadays the almost universal practice is for the captain to control his party by word of mouth. What we may have lost in pageantry and military precision we have undoubtedly gained in simplicity and clarity.

At the back of the group there will be a " second in command ", who will warn the riders when they are about to be overtaken by some other vehicle, so that they may not needlessly impede the passage of faster traffic. For the same reason cycling clubs are normally split up into groups of convenient size when they are out on the road, so that any overtaking vehicle may pass a particular group and pull into the side of the road behind the next group to allow any approaching traffic to go by. It is also the job of the man at the back to give clear signals to traffic behind him.

Easier and Happier

On their week-end runs cycling clubs normally travel somewhat faster than the individual riders would do if they were on their own, and as a rule they also cover greater distances. Nevertheless, the riders are less tired at the end of the day than if they had ridden at the same speed or covered the same distance alone.

That is one of the rather surprising features of cycling-club life. It is a psychological effect. The individual members of the group are not handicapped by those uneasy doubts which sometimes throw the lone rider into a state of fatigue that is really a form of despair. Many a young rider who could not accomplish eighty miles in a day on his own has found that he can do more than a hundred when riding with a group of similar people. It is, however, important that the group should be composed of cyclists of similar ability and similar outlook. A youngster who tries to keep up with a group of hard riders, whose capacity is far beyond his own, will gain nothing, and may suffer considerably by the end of the day.

Most cycling clubs arrange half-day runs for Saturdays and full-day outings for Sundays. In addition, they usually organise, for those of their members who are interested, long week-end tours at Whitsuntide and the August Bank holiday, and probably a full-length tour of two (or even three) weeks during the summer months. Many clubs now have sections affiliated to the Youth Hostels Association, and so can organise holiday tours on very cheap lines. Within the ranks of the C.T.C. there are, of course, a number of local sections offering special facilities such as appeal to youth hostellers, campers, hard riders, photographers and (in some districts) family parties.

It can be said, in fact, that every kind of cyclist can find a club to suit him.

CHAPTER XVII

FUN AND GAMES

CYCLING-CLUB life is not restricted to those occasions when the members go riding in groups along the lanes and by-roads. Week-end runs of that kind are usually interspersed with competitions of one sort or another, events which give an extra spice of variety to an already happily varied life.

In addition, in winter all the popular cycling clubs organise indoor attractions, and most of them have regular clubroom meetings. There members assemble for games, competitions, lantern lectures, film shows, dances and so on.

Lantern lectures are a very popular item in cycling-club life. Most cycle tourists are keen photographers, and quite a number of them are willing to go to the trouble of preparing slides so that they may give cycling audiences an account of their travels. In that way many young riders who otherwise might not have thought of going in for extensive touring have been introduced to one of the happiest forms of holiday available to them.

Nowadays the use of the cine camera is becoming more general, and cycling-club audiences are frequently offered some very interesting programmes of travel talks illustrated by films (quite often in colour).

Indoor competitions for winter evenings in the club-room may vary from darts tournaments to the recognition of well-known advertisements from small features displayed anonymously on the walls. Whist drives, beetle drives and other card contests are naturally popular, as are table tennis, draughts, dominoes and—just ordinary plain chin-wagging, chatting among old cronies, recalling past rides and planning others for the future.

Out of doors the fun and games available to cycling-club members are almost unlimited in their variety. There are treasure hunts, map-reading contests, paper (or chalk) chases, tourist trials and the less spectacular but none-the-less popular standard rides.

Treasure Hunt

In its simplest form the treasure hunt is often given the curiously mixed and discouraging name of " scaveng-ing hunt ". The essential idea of this kind of competition is that each entrant shall be given a list of articles to be collected during the course of the afternoon or day. Marks are awarded to the hunters according to the estimated difficulty of finding the various objects. Naturally the success of the event depends to a great extent on the imagination (and perhaps the sense of humour) of the organiser. In some cases the com-petitors operate individually, in others they work as small teams.

Competitions of this kind can be varied very con-siderably to suit the local circumstances and the interest of the competitors themselves. The event could be restricted, for instance, to the collection of specimens of plants and flowers. On another occasion the articles to be " collected " might be data of topographical or architectural interest. In that case the entrants would be given not merely a list of articles to be collected but a series of questions to be answered, each question relating to some feature of the countryside which must be visited in the search for the right answer.

The answering of questions, rather than the collecting of miscellaneous articles, is the basis of more than one variation of the treasure-hunt theme. In a typical example the riders are given, at the starting point, a sealed envelope containing a clue to the situation of the first of a series of check points. Then as each com-petitor arrives at that check point he is given another clue, so that he may find the second one. On his way to the second check point he must answer a question contained in his clue sheet, a question that can only be answered correctly after intelligent study of the vicinity of the first check point.

In that way the entrants proceed from one check point to another, collecting a series of questions and answers on the way, until they eventually reach the end of the trail, where, in theory at least, the ultimate treasure lies buried. They receive marks for the accuracy of the answers given to the questions, and also for the speed with which they completed the course.

Map-reading Contests

A development of the fundamental idea of the treasure hunt is the map-reading contest, in which entrants are given clues that are generally less enigmatic than those devised for treasure hunts, but call for a fair measure of map-reading skill in their solution. The riders must, of course, all be using the same kind of map —the one-inch Ordnance Survey is generally considered best for the purpose, because it shows topographical features in detail and yet covers a large enough area of ground.

Competitors are despatched at regular intervals from the starting point, and have to make their way by the route they consider most expeditious to the various check points. The winner is the one who completes the course in the shortest time.

In one very interesting variation of the map-reading idea the competitors do not equip themselves with a prescribed map. In fact, they are forbidden to carry any maps of their own. Instead, at the start of the competition each of them is given an outline map of the competition area which shows all the roads, rivers, railway lines, woods and so on, but does not give the names of towns or villages or rivers and does not indicate by means of the usual conventional signs the positions of churches, inns and post offices. At appropriate places on the map there are numbers corresponding to the numbers on a list of questions which is given to each entrant at the same time as he receives the map.

The starting point of the competition is shown on the map, and each entrant has to make his own way, by whatever route he thinks best, from point to point to enable him to answer the questions on his list. Typical questions are:

1. " Is this a church or a post office? "
2. " Does the railway cross the road by a bridge or a level crossing? "
3. " What is the name of this inn? "
4. " What kind of tree is growing between the church door and the churchyard gate? "
5. " What colour is the door of the grocer's shop? "

Here again the success of the competition depends very largely on the imagination and draughtsmanship of the organiser. There is no doubt, however, that a well-run competition of this kind gives a great deal of pleasure to the entrants and encourages them to use their powers of observation.

Twenty Questions

Observation and the answering of questions are the basis of another competition, but in this case the entrants do not have to find their own way round the course, and speed is not an essential factor in the event. At the start of the competition they are given a list of twenty questions (possibly made slightly more difficult to answer by being couched in crossword clue phraseology). They are then allowed five minutes to study the questions before setting off, as an ordinary club run, under the leadership of the organiser. He is the only one who knows the route to be followed.

The course has been chosen so that, in passing along it, the riders will find (if they are sufficiently observant) the answers to their questions (but not necessarily in the order in which they are listed). A moderate speed is set by the leader, so that the riders may stop and fill in answers to questions when they feel so inclined without risk of missing the main group. The shrewder entrants will, of course, do their clerical work some distance after they have observed something to which a question refers. Otherwise they merely draw their companions' attention to their discovery.

Paper Chases

No reputable cycling club organises a paper chase in its original form. That is to say, the hares (the riders laying the trail) do not scatter paper about the countryside. Instead they leave less obtrusive clues at appropriate points along their route. The clues may be small splashes of dye or little paper arrows pinned to trees or fences.

Tourist Trials

Most attractive of all outdoor cycling competitions, but the one calling for most skill and care in the organisation, is the tourist trial. It is essentially a series of related contests, designed to test the rider's ability in several directions, and also taking into account the condition in which he maintains his bicycle.

Entrants are despatched along a prescribed route (indicated on a card which they must carry) and have to check in at certain indicated places. In addition, they are observed secretly at other places, so that their general roadmanship may be observed and assessed. Penalties are imposed for faults (either by deducting points from a credit of 100 with which every entrant starts or by allocating a reduced number of marks instead of the possible allowance at each stage).

Often a speed-judging test is included. In that case the riders are required to maintain a stipulated average speed throughout a part of the ride, and at the end they

are marked on their success in that respect. Of course,
the carrying of watches is forbidden.

A typical trial, as carried out by one of the district
associations of the Cyclists' Touring Club, includes a
map-reading test, a hill climb, a rough ride, a brake test,
a speed-judging test and a general quiz, as well as provision for observing and marking roadmanship and the
mechanical condition of the bicycles.

In the map-reading test the riders have to check in at
five places, and are given marks for each check. They
lose marks if this part of the test takes longer than a
stipulated time. For the hill climb a stiffish gradient is
divided into three sections, and the entrants are given
marks for ascending, without putting their feet to the
ground, one or all of the sections. The rough ride
is done on a short stretch of very tricky surface
(either stony, rutty, or muddy or perhaps all three), and
here again the course is split up into sections, so that the
rider who covers the whole of it without putting a foot to
the ground gains the maximum possible number of
marks.

For a brake test it is necessary to give the riders a
signal to pull up at a place where they did not expect it.
If they are unable to do so before any part of the bicycle
crosses a white tape, they lose marks. Marks are, of
course, awarded for all the separate ingredients in this
very enjoyable and attractive form of competition.

Standard Rides

Standard rides are events in which the entrants'
ability to ride a set distance within a stipulated time is
tested. Strictly speaking, they are not competitions,
and no individual entrant is declared the winner. Instead, everybody who completes the course in the
allotted time is given a certificate or badge as a proof
that he has attained the given standard.

Events of this kind are especially popular among the
district associations of the C.T.C., and the standard

most commonly aimed at is the "100 in 8". To achieve it the riders must cover 100 miles in eight hours. If they take longer than eight hours they fail in their attempt to obtain a certificate, and if they cover the distance in less than eight hours they are not credited with their extra speed. In fact, everything possible is done to discourage entrants from trying to improve on the standard for which they have entered.

By agreement between the C.T.C. and the Road Times Trials Council (see page 149), no event may be promoted "which necessitates maintenance by the participants of average riding speeds in excess of 15 miles an hour ".

The entrants for a standard ride are divided into groups of convenient size, so as not to interfere with other road users, and each group is led by someone appointed by the organisers. The leader's duty is to see that members of his group ride in an orderly manner, not more than two abreast, and that they " extend all reasonable courtesy and facilities to other road users ".

The various groups are despatched at intervals of not less than five minutes, and are taken by the leaders over the prescribed course at speeds intended to bring them to the finish no more than half an hour before the end of the allotted time. The leaders have therefore a very responsible task, and must be experienced enough to be able to assess the difficulties of the course itself and the effect of the existing weather conditions, so that at no stage of the journey is the pace unduly forced, with the result that time has to be killed later on.

Riders taking part in standard rides have to wear ordinary touring costume, and their machines must be in sound mechanical condition.

Obviously a standard ride carried out in a hilly district may be in reality a stiffer test than one that is nominally similar but organised in easier country. The standards are not in any way national, and the value of the certificates or badges awarded is purely local. Nevertheless, they are keenly sought after by members of C.T.C. district associations, who take a quiet pride in thus measuring their ability as cyclists and finding it " not so bad ".

Brevets

Somewhat similar to the British standard rides are the various *brevet* trials organised by cycling clubs in France and Switzerland.

Like the standard rides, they are tests in which the entrants are called upon to cover a stipulated distance in a given time, but generally the routes chosen are quite difficult.

Some of those carried out in alpine districts are indeed gruelling contests, and although in theory the entrants do not benefit in any way by covering the course in less than the stipulated time, in practice there may be keen competition to be first home, even though no one is allowed to " sign off " until an hour before the close of the event. The riders travel individually, and not in groups, and so it is necessary to arrange for them to be checked at appropriate places en route.

In the *brevet* rides, as in the standard rides, the successful entrants receive a certificate or badge as proof of their ability to reach the required standard. Prizes, as such, are never awarded, because the events are not competitions, and there are no winners in the accepted sense—only those who succeed and those who fail.

CHAPTER XVIII

CYCLE RACING

NONE of the competitions mentioned in the previous chapter can be described as a road race, although fast riding by the entrants is a factor contributing to success in some of them, such as the map-reading contests and treasure hunts. The only type of event in which the rider's speed is the one essential factor is the standard ride, but, as already pointed out, the average speed necessary in those rides is limited to fifteen miles an hour.

This limitation was adopted by agreement between the C.T.C. and the R.T.T.C. in order to prevent the organisation of events in which the entrants would have to ride in group formation at speeds which were considered unreasonable and unsafe.

There was at that time an almost universal belief in the cycling world that anything in the nature of organised racing in group formation on British roads was thoroughly undesirable. Right up to 1952 it was agreed among the cycling organisations affiliated to the National Committee on Cycling that open racing on the roads, although common and indeed popular in other countries, was unacceptable in Britain, because it was likely to arouse public hostility and induce the authorities to legislate against every kind of road racing, including time trials, an extremely popular form of amateur road racing devised solely for the benefit of the riders and not as a public spectacle.

Time Trials

In time trials the riders do not set off together in a bunch. They are released by a starter at minute intervals and follow a course that is carefully marshalled by officials, who, at each turning, are not only respon-

sible for indicating the route to be taken by the competitors, but are also expected to see that no danger
arises from the presence of other traffic.

Most of the trials are held at a time when there is very
little traffic on the roads. The twenty-five-mile and
fifty-mile events are normally held in the early hours of
Sunday mornings, and very few people indeed, beyond
those actively concerned, know anything about them.
Longer trials, such as those over 100 miles or for periods
of twelve or twenty-four hours, naturally cannot be
completed before normal Sunday traffic begins to appear
on the roads. Nevertheless, in these cases, too, every
possible precaution is taken to see that the trials do not
attract public notice or interfere with ordinary traffic.

The routes, or courses as they are usually called, for
these events are not chosen haphazardly. In the first
place, they must obviously be carefully measured, but
that is not the only consideration. So far as possible
level courses are sought after, so that performances at
the same distance in different parts of the country may
reasonably be compared. Large centres of traffic or
population are avoided, and the routes are selected so
that the finishing point is reasonably near to the start.
That is not merely helpful to the organisers, but is also a
means of ensuring that the riders do an " out and home
ride ", so that if they get the benefit of wind assistance
in one direction, it is discounted over another part of the
course.

There are so many time trials being held in Britain
every week-end from spring to autumn, although the
general public knows little about them, that the selection
and use of courses have to be carefully supervised and
controlled by the Road Time Trials Council.

The R.T.T.C. came into existence in 1922, being then
known as the Road Racing Council. In 1938 its name
was changed to the Road Time Trials Council, and the
change of title may in itself be regarded as a reflection
of the uneasiness that has prevailed in this country for

over half a century on the subject of racing on the public roads.

Development of Road Racing

To understand the present position it is necessary to go back to the early days of cycling and trace the subsequent development. Originally there was only one national cycling organisation in this country interested in cycling sport. It was the National Cyclists' Union, established in 1878 as the Bicycle Union. The Union originally controlled all forms of racing, including record breaking, on the roads and on tracks. Within ten years of its foundation, however, the Union decided to abandon its interests in road racing, as the general belief among the leaders of cycling opinion in those days was that every form of fast cycling on the road should be condemned. From that date until 1952 the Union had no effective interest in any form of racing on roads open to the general public. Nevertheless, it was the only British cycling body recognised by the Union Cycliste Internationale.

When the Union ceased to be responsible for the supervision of attempts at record breaking, a new body known as the Road Records Association came into existence. It still exists, and carries out its work of checking and certifying records on a perfectly satisfactory voluntary basis. No corresponding body was formed to take charge of road racing as such, and the various cycling clubs interested in that sport were left to their own devices.

In view of the popular belief that ordinary road racing (nowadays described as massed start racing) should be abandoned, the clubs adopted the time-trials system already described. In that way road sport was able to develop without interference with normal traffic and without attracting public hostility. The time-trials system enabled the cyclists with an interest in road racing to compete one against the other on a strictly amateur basis, each doing his best to beat the times set up by the others (or his own previous performances) while in fact riding alone.

After the First World War the number of clubs promoting time trials became so great that the need was felt for a governing body to supervise and standardise the racing conditions. In 1922 the Road Racing Council was set up, and continued under that title for sixteen years. By that time, however, it was thought by many people interested in time trialling that the term "road racing" was inappropriate and probably dangerous, in that it might attract unwelcome attention from the authorities, who were generally regarded as being hostile to cycle racing on the public roads.

Official Attitude

That belief was strengthened by authoritative pronouncements such as the report of the Committee on Road Safety to the Minister of Transport issued in 1947, which included the following statement:

"In paragraph 115 of our interim report we expressed the view that massed start cycle racing is likely to give rise to danger, both to those participating in the events, and to other road users. We recommended that the Ministry of Transport, Home Office and Scottish Home Department should discourage this form of cycle racing, and that if their efforts did not achieve the desired result consideration should be given to the introduction of stronger measures.

"Massed start cycle races continue to be organised in this country. We see no reason to modify our earlier views and recommendations on the undesirability of this form of cycle racing, and we have accordingly considered the measures which might be introduced to deal with massed start cycle racing as distinct from time trials. In our view it is important that nothing should be done which might interfere with cycling events which do not give rise to danger or inconvenience to other road

in the LLYFNANT VALLEY
Cardiganshire

users, and we are of opinion, therefore, that any new legislation to deal with the problem should be directed to the dangerous or inconsiderate use of the roads by cyclists and not to the specific form of activity in which the cyclists are engaged."

Other similar official utterances gave apparent confirmation to the belief of the R.T.T.C. and the N.C.U. that any ordinary form of racing on the public roads would be condemned by the Ministry of Transport and the Home Office, and that attempts to introduce that sport into this country would inevitably provoke new restrictive legislation which might adversely affect other forms of cycling.

That is why the N.C.U. and the R.T.T.C., with the support of the cycle trade and other cycling organisations not directly interested in cycle racing, continuously resisted the demands of a small number of cyclists who wished to promote in this country the same kind of road racing as has always existed on the Continent.

The N.C.U. confined its attention to racing on tracks and a small number of road races on circuits closed to the public. The R.T.T.C. continued to pursue its object of " providing a national uniformity in the conduct of events and taking any steps which may be necessary to ensure the continuance and well being of the sport "— the sport being, of course, time trialling. Whenever, for international events, it was necessary to bring time trials under the supervision of the U.C.I., which recognises only the N.C.U. in this country, it was done by friendly agreement between the N.C.U. and the R.T.T.C.

B.L.R.C.

During the Second World War another cycle-racing organisation came into existence. The British League of Racing Cyclists had been formed, as a " dissident body ", with the object of promoting and controlling road racing on the Continental pattern on British roads. The sponsors of the B.L.R.C. did not agree that massed start racing was necessarily dangerous, nor did they accept the belief that had been generally held for something like half a century that racing on British roads was of doubtful legality. They themselves believed that, if properly organised in collaboration with the police, road events of the Continental kind could be held in this country with advantage to the cycling sport and industry, and moreover that massed start races would in time become as popular over here as they are in France, where crowds line the roads to see the riders pass.

Believing as they did that the authorities would not take action to stop cycle racing on the roads, the leaders of the B.L.R.C. themselves organised a number of events, which did undoubtedly attract public attention. Although the Ministry of Transport continued to " warn " the N.C.U. that the official attitude towards massed start racing was unchanged and that if the N.C.U. were to yield to popular demand and organise events of that kind the result could only be unfortunate, the B.L.R.C. went on its way successfully promoting massed start road races. In that it was assisted by one or two cycle manufacturers who did not accept their union's views on massed start racing, and also by an influential daily newspaper.

Riders who took part in the B.L.R.C. events were " suspended " by the N.C.U., and there was open (and at times bitter) disagreement between the two bodies. In 1951 a tour of Britain, on the lines of the famous Tour de France, was promoted by the B.L.R.C. with the assistance of a newspaper and some cycle manufacturers. It was successful, and no dire consequences, such as had been vaguely threatened by the Ministry of Transport over the preceding years, supervened. Instead it became obvious that the British public could be interested in cycle racing.

Soon afterwards the N.C.U. decided that it could no longer resist the demands of those who believed that massed start racing was a desirable sport and that the

N.C.U., as the official British racing-control body
affiliated to the U.C.I., should be the organisation to
promote and supervise such events. It therefore
decided to take road racing under its wing once more.

It is still too early (in 1952) to forecast the future.
Perhaps in due course the people of Britain will become
as keenly interested in cycle racing as are the French
public, and perhaps British motorists will show the same
friendly tolerance as do French drivers when directed
by the police to halt at the roadside until the competitors in a cycle race have passed. If that is so, the
result will be beneficial to cycling as a whole. On the
other hand, it is not yet possible to say definitely whether
the authorities will react in the way implied by the
Ministry of Transport during the period when it was
" persuading " the N.C.U.

The present position is that cycling clubs in Britain
are continuing to promote time trials, under the general
control of the R.T.T.C., and the N.C.U. is adding
massed start road racing to the track-racing facilities
which it has provided for more than seventy years.

Even if massed start racing does develop into the
commercially sponsored public spectacle which the newspapers and cycle-makers who are at present supporting
it naturally expect, the amateur cyclist " bitten by the
speed bug " will still make his debut in the racing world
as a competitor in some event organised by his local
club—probably a time trial, but possibly a track event.

Membership of a club that provides racing facilities
is indeed essential to any rider who would like to take up
that sport. Quite apart from the exigencies of R.T.T.C.
affiliation and N.C.U. licensing, membership of a
suitable club is necessary, because it is there that the
racing aspirant will get the advice and assistance he
needs—especially the assistance, for the racing lads are
a most friendly lot.

Cyclists Take Care

A code of cycling conduct approved and issued by the
Cyclists' Touring Club, 3 Craven Hill, London, W.2

THE LAW requires that you

Carry on your machine, when cycling during the hours of
darkness, two lamps—one showing a white light to the front,
and the other a red light to the rear.

Carry a white front light also on the sidecar, if one is attached
to your cycle, when riding at night.

Do not hold on to other vehicles unless you have lawful authority
or reasonable cause.

Give way to pedestrians at all pedestrian crossings not controlled
by police or light signals.

Obey traffic signals whether you are riding or wheeling your
machine.

Go slowly or come to a stop before entering a major road from
a minor road if there is a traffic sign requiring you to do so.

THE HIGHWAY CODE exhorts you to

Keep as near to the left as practicable unless about to overtake
or turn to the right.

Avoid riding too many abreast and thus impeding other traffic.

Be able always to pull up within the distance for which you can
see the road is clear.

Overtake only on the right, except when a driver in front has
signalled his intention to turn to the right. (Subject to any
local provisions to the contrary, tramcars may be overtaken on
either side.)

Avoid overtaking at a pedestrian crossing, at cross-roads or at
a blind corner.

Give the appropriate signal clearly and in good time before you
stop or slow down or change direction and when approaching
a constable or other person controlling traffic.

COMMON SENSE impels you to

See that your brakes and tyres are dependable.

Avoid cutting corners on the wrong side.

Dismount when it is risky to proceed.

Beware of skidding on greasy or muddy roads, through applying
your brakes suddenly, or through carelessly negotiating man-
holes, drain covers and tram lines.

Avoid depending on " the other fellow ".

Keep an eye on the movements of other traffic.

ORDINARY COURTESY implies that you will

Always behave towards other road users as you would like
them to behave towards you.

Always be a true sportsman.

Help to promote goodwill on the roads.

INDEX

COMING SOON

TEACH YOURSELF
MOTORING

By
DUDLEY NOBLE

TEACH YOURSELF
MOTORING

It is easy, and customary, for anyone who writes about driving technique to point out that one should always take the greatest care when in control of a car. While I unhesitatingly follow suit, I would like to go further, and assert that the day will come when every person who reads these words will, while at the wheel, pull himself up with a start and exclaim, in his inner consciousness, " I took a risk then. Thank heaven it was my lucky day and I didn't meet somebody else who was taking a risk too." I hope it *will* be a lucky day, and I hope, also, that a mental and very sincere resolve will be made, on the spot, that there is going to be one hundred per cent. attention to driving in the future.

Now, I am quite prepared to admit that some accidents are due to inexperience, and, perhaps, ignorance, rather than to carelessness or inattention. Let me at least, therefore, run through the more obvious points from which trouble arises on the road.

In the first place, the Highway Code ought to be read understandingly ; not just in superficial manner so that questions concerning it can be answered parrot fashion. The Highway Code is a very sane and common-sense manual to proper behaviour when using the road, and the purport of its instruction, permanently carried into practice, would rob the roads of a large proportion of their present danger. I will assume that every person who uses the road, either as driver or pedestrian, has done his duty and familiarised himself with the Highway Code. Let us proceed to an amplification of its advice, with special reference to what the learner-driver ought to get into his mind while he is still in that stage of his motoring education.

"Road Sense" is a very real thing, and it is a subject that can be self-taught. A person who has acquired road sense not only follows the instructions of the Highway Code *instinctively*, but develops a sort of second sight which enables him to anticipate things about to happen, and to prepare himself accordingly. Perhaps I should amend that and say "are likely to be about to happen," for, although he foresees, and prepares for, eventualities, they may not always actually come to pass.

For instance, there may be a group of children on the pavement ahead. They may be quite placid, and apparently likely to remain so. But, the driver with a fully developed road sense will find himself automatically preparing to make an emergency stop, and noting in his rear-view mirror that no vehicle is immediately behind him. If there were, he would give its driver a cautionary signal that he intended to slow down. The good driver does, indeed, pay a great amount of attention to his rear-view mirror, although he does it in such a way that it does not take his attention off the road ahead for more than the metaphorical flicker of an eyelid. He keeps himself continuously posted as to following traffic, especially in towns where he may need to move from one traffic lane to another.

On the open road, he will keep a wary eye cocked for side

turnings, and, if there are no hedges, he will glance to right and left along the intersecting road to gain an impression of whether a cyclist, a cart, or, perhaps, cattle, are to be expected. The last-named call for special attention in many parts of the country, for a cow may appear with considerable suddenness from a field path or farm lane, but the driver who has road sense will have noticed signs of their habitual presence from marks on the road or from traces in the neighbourhood.

In the same way, in mountainous districts like Wales and Scotland, sheep may be expected to materialise on the road with startling abruptness ; they will, however, be less of a shock to the driver with road sense, because he will have anticipated their presence and will always suspect that, if they are going to get in his way, they will do so at the most unexpected spot. He will, instinctively and pessimistically, assume that somebody or something will always be doing some fool thing round the corner.

When rounding a bend on a country road, he will anticipate that there will be two or three pedestrians spread out across the road and a cyclist or another car coming in the opposite direction. He will, therefore, blow his horn to signify his presence, but will not rely on this clearing his path ; he will have his car under such control that he can stop with certainty within range of his vision. But he will blow his horn to show that he is there, and in the hope that, if there should be another car coming, its driver will likewise warn of *his* presence.

As regards the use of the horn, the driver with road sense, while he does not blow it unnecessarily, or, shall I say, at places where the onus rests on him to be specially prudent, will not fail to use it as a means of signifying his presence on the road at points where that knowledge would be useful to other drivers. For example, on a narrow, twisty road, it is wise for two drivers to announce where they are when concealed one from the other. At a cross-roads where two main or semi-main roads meet, each driver should slow down to a pace from which he can bring his car to a stop, and not rely on the horn to clear his way.

It might here, perhaps, be mentioned that the rule of the road in Great Britain does not recognise priority being given to traffic coming from the right or the left of another vehicle. In certain Continental countries, notably France, there is a very strict rule that a driver gives way to another driver coming up on his right. By virtue of this, a driver has to keep a sharp watch for traffic on one side of him only, and does not, as we do in the United Kingdom, have to move his head from one side to another in order to keep a two-way look-out. It is this rule which keeps traffic moving rapidly, yet with reasonable safety, in the roundabouts of Paris and other large French towns, while to a British driver there seems danger threatening from every side. Let him follow suit, when in Paris, and he will find the traffic problem much simplified.

To return to the horn, however, there are some drivers who say with pride that they never make use of the one on their own car, and such drivers number among their ranks some of the best and most accident-free. My own personal opinion, however, is that judicious use of the horn is both necessary and desirable ; it should not be done as a command to other people to get off the road, but as a warning that one's car is approaching. It should be borne in mind that, in the event of an accident, one of the first questions a driver will be asked is : " Did you blow your horn ? " Remember that the law demands an audible warning of approach shall be given, and that, if only *one* accident can be prevented by such warning, the horn has proved its worth.

A driver who has taught himself road sense will be very particular as to where he leaves his car. If, for instance, he wishes to stop by the roadside, he will consider very carefully before coming to a standstill. If there should happen

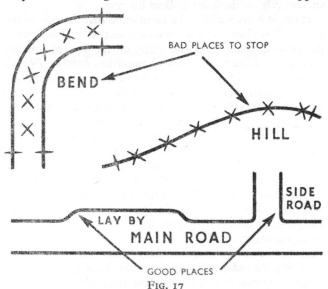

FIG. 17

The crosses denote places where a good driver will never stop his car. He will find a lay-by or a side road where his vehicle will not impede traffic flow.

to be a side road down which he could turn off the main highway, and so leave the latter clear, he will make use of it. Or, if there should be a verge on to which he could pull, he will do so. If, however, he must stop at the roadside, he will seek a stretch of road where his car will not impair the view of an oncoming driver. He would never park on a bend, or at the crest of a hill—or, worse still, just over the crest.

It is literally astonishing how many drivers lack road sense, in this connection. A car when stationary can be almost as dangerous in the hands of a bad driver as it can be when moving, yet one sees evidence every day of the gross lack of road sense with which very many drivers are afflicted. Always remember, when parking or merely stopping a car by the roadside, that every passing driver is entitled to a clear view of the road and, if your car is preventing him from having that, then you are lacking in road sense. In some countries, notably in the United States, it is an offence to stop your car on the highway, even out in the open country. You must pull on to the verge (or " soft shoulder," as it is called), and leave the traffic lane completely clear. One cannot, unfortunately, always do the same in Britain, owing to the prevalence of kerbs, but at least one should do the next best thing, which is to get out of the other fellow's line of vision.

Equally as important is care when re-starting from rest. Road sense will tell a driver that traffic coming up behind will receive a shock if his stationary car suddenly starts to move, and proceeds on into the traffic stream ; that a driver whose attention may be momentarily off the road may quite conceivably run into his back before he gathers speed. Yet it is common to see cars pull off a parking place and proceed straight on the road, with a " take care of yourself " attitude. No good driver does such a thing ; he makes a careful survey of oncoming traffic in both directions before he sets his car in motion, and, if there is a vehicle coming which he can see he will clear easily, he will still give a signal, if only as a courtesy.

Now, signalling can be overdone. One sees a great deal of unnecessary hand- and trafficator-waggling, and it is apt to be a source of irritation to other drivers. Usually it betokens that the person who is doing the signalling is inexperienced—perhaps even doing his driving test. Do not think that I am advocating against signalling ; I am merely pointing out that signals, when given, should be made clearly to inform other road users of an intention on the part of a driver which it is necessary to reveal. It is the ambiguous, unnecessary and obscure hand-waving that I am decrying.

The Highway Code lays down and illustrates four signals by which drivers of motor cars are to indicate their own intentions, and points out that these signals are for the purpose of giving information *and not instructions* to other road users. The four signals are :—

1. " I am going to slow down or stop."
2. " I am going to turn to my right."
3. " I am ready to be overtaken."
4. " I am going to turn to my left."

These are the only four recognised signals, and, if made properly, each is clear and distinctive. But how frequently does one see obscure, ambiguous and unofficial signals given ? Remember the *Punch* cartoon where a lady driver is saying to a policeman, after an accident : " But I clearly gave the signal that I had changed my mind ! "

The mechanical traffic indicator can perform only two of the four signals, the turn to the right and the turn to the left. Even in the case of the latter, it is not always wise to rely on the indicator arm conveying the message to traffic which is following at a fairly close range, since a driver who is on your tail, and possibly intending to overtake, may not be in a position to see the indicator arm on the far side of the car. In such cases, the good driver will give one of those instantaneous glances into his rear-view mirror and, if he sees that there is another vehicle close behind, he will give a hand signal as well as switch up his left-hand trafficator.

A driver with road sense will likewise use discretion as to how far he relies on his mechanical indicator to give clear and sufficient warning of his intentions. For instance, on a main road where there is fast traffic, a following driver may not be close enough to see that the indicator arm is out until it is too late to dive over to the left-hand side of the road in order to pass on the nearside while the driver who is signalling is waiting for an opportunity to turn to the right. There is also the matter of lighting conditions to be considered: I once had an unpleasant moment when, about to overtake another car on a fast stretch of arterial road, I suddenly realised that its indicator arm was out and that the driver was actually on the point of turning across the road on to a parking place. But what the good lady in charge of the car had not realised was that (a) there was no light showing inside her trafficator arm, and (b) the sun was dead ahead, fairly low in the sky, and the trafficator was almost blotted out by glare.

In such a case, a driver with well-developed road sense would have appreciated that someone was coming up behind, at a rapid pace, and needed a more clearly visible signal than even a properly-working trafficator could give, and would therefore have extended an arm to supplement the indicator.

Every car owner should, from time to time, make a check on the trafficators fitted to his vehicle, not only to see that they really are working but also to make certain that the light inside the arm is functioning. This last is highly important, because, without the glow inside the transparent red casing, a trafficator is not a very clearly visible signal.

I remember once having another narrow squeak when a car, restarting at traffic lights, suddenly pulled right across my bows and did, in fact, scrape my wing. I stopped the driver, after a chase, and asked him why he had not signalled his intention of turning. He replied that he had put out his trafficator, and, when I requested him to repeat the process, as I had certainly not seen the arm, he discovered that the arm was stuck in its recess, although the light inside it could be seen glowing when one stood by the side of the car.

The keynote of the Highway Code is " Consideration for others, as well as for yourself." If you let this sink in, you will always put yourself in the place of the other fellow, and ask yourself " Should I know what I am about to do ? " " Am I giving as much room as I can ? " " Is my car blocking his view ? " These are the things we all hope that the other driver will do for *us*, to the end that traffic may flow freely and with the maximum of safety.

And just one more point about signalling ; an exhortation to do it in good time. If you are going to turn, to stop or to slow down, let those who are following have adequate notice of your intentions. Bear in mind that the other man may possibly, at the instant you give your signal, have his attention momentarily occupied with some other detail and, therefore, if you give your signal at the very last instant, when you are on the point of carrying it into effect, he may not receive it until a fraction too late.

British mandatory signs.

British direction signs.

British prohibitory signs.

DRIVING

Prohibition of Traffic

No Entry

Customs House

No Parking

Obligatory Direction

No Waiting

Cross Roads

Dangerous Bend

Danger Ahead

Gully in Road

Gated Level Crossing

Ungated Level Crossing

International signs, used on the Continent.

British informative signs, which differ in some respects from the international code.

Join more than 60 million people

who have reached their goals with

Teach Yourself®

and never stop learning.

Launched in 1938, Teach Yourself® has helped over 60 million readers learn the skills they need to thrive in work, study and life. Now, 80 years on, there are Teach Yourself® books on everything from starting a business and learning a language to writing a novel and playing piano.

To find out more about books in the Teach Yourself® series, visit:

teachyourself.com